At Issue

Caffeine

Other Books in the At Issue Series:

At Issue

Caffeine

Amy Francis, Book Editor

GREENHAVEN PRESS
A part of Gale, Cengage Learning

GALE
CENGAGE Learning

Farmington Hills, Mich • San Francisco • New York • Waterville, Maine
Meriden, Conn • Mason, Ohio • Chicago

Judy Galens, *Manager, Frontlist Acquisitions*

For more information, contact:
Greenhaven Press
27500 Drake Rd.
Farmington Hills, MI 48331-3535
Or you can visit our Internet site at gale.cengage.com

For product information and technology assistance, contact us at

Gale Customer Support, 1-800-877-4253
For permission to use material from this text or product, submit all requests online at www.cengage.com/permissions

Further permissions questions can be e-mailed to permissionrequest@cengage.com

Articles in Greenhaven Press anthologies are often edited for length to meet page requirements. In addition, original titles of these works are changed to clearly present the main thesis and to explicitly indicate the author's opinion. Every effort is made to ensure that Greenhaven Press accurately reflects the original intent of the authors. Every effort has been made to trace the owners of copyrighted material.

Cover image © Images.com/Corbis.

LIBRARY OF CONGRESS CATALOGING-IN-PUBLICATION DATA

Francis, Amy
  Caffeine / Amy Francis.
    pages cm. -- (At issue)
  Includes bibliographical references and index.
  ISBN 978-0-7377-7380-4 (hbk.) -- ISBN 978-0-7377-7381-1 (pbk.)
  1. Caffeine--Juvenile literature. I. Title.
  QP801.C24.F73 2015
  613.8'4--dc23
                                                    2015023350

Printed in Mexico
1 2 3 4 5 6 7 19 18 17 16

Contents

Introduction

Just a few grams of caffeine powder can be lethal, yet it is completely legal, inexpensive, and readily available for purchase online and through some health stores. When used appropriately, consumers mix a small amount of the powder with liquid to make their own energy drinks. Misuse, however, has been linked to numerous deaths and thousands of emergency room visits and poison control center calls. The reason powdered caffeine has been allowed to remain on the market despite its potential for misuse is that powdered caffeine, unlike the caffeine found in energy drinks, colas, coffee, tea, or chocolate, is not regulated by the US Food and Drug Administration (FDA) as a food ingredient. It is sold as a dietary supplement, which places it in a different category of regulation.

Since the passage of the Dietary Supplement and Health and Education Act (DSHEA), approved by Congress in 1994, herbal supplements and botanicals are exempted as dietary supplements. As a result, these products do not require the manufacturer to seek approval from the FDA prior to being marketed and sold. The manufacturers and distributers themselves are solely responsible for making sure their products are safe before they land on store shelves.

Donald M. Marcus of Baylor College of Medicine and Arthur P. Grollman of Stony Brook University explain the situation as follows:

> Even when the agency [FDA] identifies an unsafe product, it lacks authority to mandate its removal from the market because it must meet the very high legal requirement to demonstrate a "significant or unreasonable" risk. That is why it took the FDA more than 10 years to remove from the mar-

ket ephedra-containing herbal weight-loss products that had caused hundreds of deaths and thousands of adverse events.[1]

Ephedra or ephedrine (also known as *Ma-huang*) was traditionally used in Chinese medicine to treat a variety of illnesses, including asthma, colds and flu, and fever. In the early 1990s in the United States, ephedrine quickly became a popular dietary supplement for weight loss and increased energy. In 1993, however, the FDA began receiving reports of adverse events allegedly associated with the supplement.

After a decade of issuing repeated warnings about the potential hazards of using products containing ephedrine, numerous studies, and legislative action, the FDA was finally able to release its final rule declaring "dietary supplements containing ephedrine alkaloids to be adulterated under the Federal Food, Drug, and Cosmetic Act."[2] The ruling, which prohibited the sale of ephedrine-containing dietary supplements, went into effect on April 12, 2004. As a result, ephedrine-containing products were removed from the market, and many companies reformulated their supplements to contain ephedrine alternatives.

The ephedrine alternative many manufacturers turned to is the substance DMAA (1,3-dimethylamylamine, sometimes referred to as geranium extract), and DMAA was widely added to products marketed for sports performance and weight loss. Proponents argue that DMAA is available in geraniums and is therefore a natural compound. Opponents and the FDA maintain that there is no strong scientific evidence to support the claim that DMAA exists naturally in the geranium plant. The FDA states that the DMAA used in the products is synthetic—

1. Donald M. Marcus and Arthur P. Grollman, "The Consequences of Ineffective Regulation of Dietary Supplements," *Archives of Internal Medicine*, July 9, 2012.
2. US Food and Drug Administration, *Final Rule Declaring Dietary Supplements Containing Ephedrine Alkaloids Adulterated Because They Present an Unreasonable Risk*, July 17, 2008. http://www.fda.gov/Food/GuidanceRegulation/GuidanceDocuments RegulatoryInformation/DietarySupplements/ucm072997.htm.

not extracted from the geranium plant. As such, the FDA argues, DMAA is an illegal additive.

Manufacturers disagree. A spokesman for USPLabs, quoted in an article at nutraingredients-USA.com, states that "DMAA is, in fact, a constituent of geranium ... and has been consumed as part of the human diet for more than 100 years ... what is currently in circulation about the ingredient is speculation and conjecture."[3]

As for consumers, a natural bodybuilder named Perez, quoted in the *Chicago Tribune*, states, "Before I found DMAA, I used to stop at the gas station and get either two (Monster Energy Drinks) or two Red Bulls. How healthy could that have been? It was like drinking buckets of sugar."[4]

Energy drinks have in fact put the issue of caffeine consumption back under the spotlight. The health benefits and potential dangers of energy drinks, along with the more popular coffee, tea, and colas, are debated in the following pages of *At Issue: Caffeine.*

3. Quoted in Elaine Watson, "USPLabs: DMAA Is from Geranium Oil—and Critics Are 'Uninformed,'" nutraingredients-USA.com, January 5, 2012. www.nutraingredients-usa.com/Regulation/USPLabs-DMAA-is-from-geranium-oil-and-critics-are-uninformed.
4. Quoted in Julie Deardorff, "Pressure Builds to Ban Dietary Supplement DMAA," *Chicago Tribune*, June 4, 2012. http://articles.chicagotribune.com/2012-06-04/news/ct-met-dmaa-supplements-20120604_1_dietary-ingredient-supplements-safety-concerns/2.

1

Caffeine Has Many Health Benefits

Nancy Maleki

Nancy Maleki is an independent health writer and frequent contributor to HealthRX.

There is strong evidence supporting coffee's health benefits, particularly in the areas of cognitive function and neurological conditions such as Parkinson's Disease. Other benefits include better mental health and a lowered risk of diabetes and some cancers. In some studies it appears that the caffeine in coffee is responsible for the health benefits; however, it's unclear if the caffeine is solely responsible or the health benefits are from the other components in coffee. While some caution should be taken due to the risk of side effects, coffee can be part of a healthy diet.

If your preferred morning beverage is a cup of strong coffee, you have plenty of company. But is that cup of java really a good choice health-wise?

Research has shown coffee to have varying effects on health. Some studies have shown that drinking coffee may destroy gallstones and lower the risk for prostate cancer and diabetes. Other studies, however, have revealed that coffee may increase cholesterol and blood pressure.

Coffee's Benefits

The experts disagree on whether something so widely enjoyed can really be so good for you, but several recent studies suggest that may be the case. Here we explore the possible top five health benefits of coffee.

Parkinson's Disease. Parkinson's disease is a neurodegenerative disorder that results from damage to a region of the midbrain called the substantia nigra. This damage can lead to tremors, difficulty walking, and later on, mental decline. Recent studies have suggested that the onset of Parkinson's (usually around age 50) is delayed by coffee and that the motor issues (body movement) associated with the disease may improve with drinking coffee. Coffee has even been shown to prevent Parkinson's.

Back in 2000, a study led by G. Webster Ross, MD, of the Department of Veterans Affairs in Honolulu, Hawaii, that appeared in *JAMA* [*Journal of the American Medical Association*] found that the higher the caffeine intake, the lower the incidence of Parkinson's disease. This study linked this effect to caffeine itself rather than other nutrients in coffee.

There are questions as to whether women benefit from coffee as much as men when it comes to Parkinson's disease. In a 2001 prospective study of caffeine consumption and risk of Parkinson's disease in men and women that appeared in the *Annals of Neurology* (by [Alberto] Ascherio et al), the researchers suggested that hormones may decrease the effect of caffeine on the risk for Parkinson's in women.

Research . . . has suggested that coffee may help keep young people from being distracted.

Improvement in Cognitive Functioning. Several studies have suggested that coffee may improve memory and other brain functioning. This effect seems to be particularly true for the elderly and for women.

According to the European Food Safety Authority, the amount of caffeine in one regular cup of coffee (about 75 mg [milligrams]) improves alertness and concentration.

Some studies have suggested that if you regularly drink coffee, you may build up a tolerance and need more to achieve this effect.

Research also has suggested that coffee may help keep young people from being distracted.

Some studies have suggested that a few ounces (6 to 8 ounces) of coffee throughout the day is what works best, and others say too much coffee can work in the opposite way and make a person who drinks too much become jittery and less able to concentrate.

A 2010 study in *Appetite* (by [E.A.] De Bruin et al) found that tea also improved attention and alertness. Other studies have suggested that decaffeinated coffee also may work, if only that it might offer a placebo effect (not real but imagined), i.e., if you think it can cause you to be more alert, you may actually become more alert.

Less Depression. Three studies by Harvard researchers found that people who drink coffee may be less likely to commit suicide.

A study by Harvard School of Public Health researchers found that women who drank four cups of coffee a day were 20 percent less likely to be depressed. This study found that any source of caffeine conferred the same benefit.

Diabetes. Several studies have suggested that drinking coffee may reduce diabetes risk. In a study that appeared in the *American Journal of Clinical Nutrition*, during the more than 20 years of follow-up, coffee consumption, regardless of caffeine content, was associated with an 8 percent decreased risk of type 2 diabetes in women. In men, the reduction was 4 percent for regular coffee and 7 percent for decaf.

It seems that the more coffee an individual drinks (up to 6-8 cups per day), the lower their risk for diabetes may be.

In one Harvard University study, increasing coffee consumption by an average of one and a half cups per day reduced a caffeine drinker's risk of developing type 2 diabetes by 11 percent.

One study that appeared in *Diabetes Care* suggested that in people who already have diabetes, drinking coffee may make it harder to control blood sugar. According to that study, caffeine seemed to increase insulin resistance (insulin is released by the pancreas, but the body doesn't use it properly, so blood sugars aren't lowered as they should be). Therefore, a person with diabetes who expects their glucose to be low based on what they have eaten may find it's high because the caffeine they ingested did not allow insulin to do its job.

Other studies have shown that decaffeinated tea or coffee also may protect against type 2 diabetes (the type of diabetes caused by insulin resistance).

Lower Risk for Certain Cancers. Several studies have suggested that prostate cancer, liver cancer and endometrial cancer may be prevented or reduced by the intake of coffee.

In one study in the *Journal of the National Cancer Institute*, men who drank the most coffee reduced their risk of getting the most lethal form of prostate cancer by about 60 percent compared to the men who drank the least amount of coffee.

Coffee may offer some protection [from diseases and ailments], and moderate consumption is always a good choice.

Coffee has also been linked to lower rates of liver cancer in several studies, including one by [W.W.] Leung et al that showed that the incidence of hepatocellular carcinoma was reduced by 30 to 80 percent among coffee drinkers (the difference dependent on how much coffee was consumed).

A study that appeared in *Cancer Epidemiology, Biomarkers & Prevention* also revealed evidence that drinking coffee may cut the risk of endometrial (uterine) cancer. The researchers found this effect when women drank four or more cups of coffee per day.

Concerns and Complications

Coffee also has been associated with reduced rates of gallstones, liver disease and other ailments. As with all the conditions listed here, coffee may offer some protection, and moderate consumption is always a good choice, particularly if you have high blood pressure (coffee is known to increase blood pressure), a stomach ulcer (coffee can hurt these openings in the lining of the stomach) or other heart issues (caffeine makes the heart beat faster).

In many of these studies, the researchers pointed out that it is hard to be sure if these associations are with coffee, and not other lifestyle factors that participants shared. For example, are coffee drinkers more likely to smoke or to eat healthily? Could they exercise more or worry less than people who don't drink coffee?

There are many ingredients in coffee, so what is working against one condition may not be what is working against another.

The American Medical Association Council on Scientific Affairs states that moderate tea or coffee drinking is not likely to be harmful to your health as long as you have other good health habits.

According to Deborah Gordon, MD, a homeopathy and nutrition expert, "As a practitioner who has spent years advising coffee avoidance, I am also someone who keeps abreast of current nutritional research, and there is no denying the numerous studies validating the health benefits of coffee."

Dr. Gordon told *dailyRx News*, "Some uncertainties remain, however, such as the question of discerning the separate effects of coffee vs. caffeine. Caffeine-induced adrenaline se-cretion, for instance, helps release fat from body stores and boosts insulin resistance to allow that fat to be burned as fuel, yet coffee itself is linked to lower body weight, lowered insulin resistance and protection from type 2 diabetes. I believe that apparent dilemma reflects the difference between acute and chronic effects, and have in common the beneficial mobiliza-tion of stored fat."

There are other aspects that make the controversy more difficult, she noted. "Additional confounding issues include the effects of rare vs. habituated coffee or caffeine intake, and the undeniable pleasure of a sweet treat taken with your coffee and cream—which can easily undo all the benefit you might derive from the coffee. I would suggest you drink the coffee, with organic whole cream is best, and let its effects satiate any cravings you have for sweets: pass on the pastries!" she said.

"If you don't like the caffeine effect, you can still benefit from coffee's many other components, so enjoy decaf. If you don't like the flavor at all, tea has also been shown to confer some of the same health benefits, though not all."

2

Death by Caffeine Really Is a Thing If You're Susceptible

Ian Musgrave

Ian Musgrave is a senior lecturer in pharmacology at the University of Adelaide, in Australia.

Although caffeine-related deaths are exceedingly rare, they do occur. Some individuals are more susceptible to caffeine because of existing health conditions or a lowered ability of the body to process caffeine efficiently. It is important that manufacturers of products containing caffeine prominently display consumer alerts on their packaging to alert consumers that the products contain caffeine and that excessive caffeine consumption can be dangerous. More needs to be done to make caffeine-related deaths even more rare.

Sadly, tragic news has emerged that a man in the United Kingdom recently died from caffeine overdose. John Jackson was 40 years old.

What makes this unfortunate death worrying is that it was due to consumption of caffeine-laced mints. Misfortune can strike us in many ways, but we generally don't expect a tin of sweeties to be our downfall.

I've written about death by caffeine before, but this particular tragedy involves a different aspect of one of the key themes of my blog and toxicology generally—the dose makes the poison.

How Much Is Too Much?

Everyone knows that caffeine is a stimulant and heightens alertness; this caffeine boost is part of the pleasurable effect of a good cup of coffee.

Caffeine also makes the heart beat faster and stronger, and high concentrations can cause severe heart problems (among other things), and even death. But despite widespread consumption of caffeine-containing drinks and caffeine pills, death by caffeine overdose is extraordinarily rare.

In this particular case, the deceased had consumed an entire tin of caffeine-containing mints. Each individual mint contained 80 milligrams of caffeine, about the same amount as in some moderate-level energy drinks.

Consuming the whole tin of the mints is like consuming 12 cans of a moderate-level energy drink, one after the other.

But is that enough to kill you? The handy website Death by Caffeine, where you can find out how many cans of energy drink, cups of coffee or bars of chocolate you will need to consume before expiring, suggests that a 70-kilogram person would need to drink 132 cans of a beverage containing 80 milligrams of caffeine (or a similar number of shots of espresso coffee) to die of an overdose.

Some people are more susceptible to caffeine intoxication.

If that's correct, then Jackson should have had a tenfold safety margin, so what went wrong?

Underlying Susceptibilities

Sensitivity to caffeine and our ability to break it down varies between people. A recent report about energy drinks in the *MJA* [*Medical Journal of Australia*] found that people drinking no more than the recommended amount of energy drinks showed significant signs of toxicity (such as palpitations, and even parts of their heart muscle dying).

No one featured in the report actually died, but the average caffeine-containing energy drink consumption of people presenting to the emergency department was between three and eight cans.

These levels are on the threshold of caffeine intoxication, and should only be associated with mild symptoms. They demonstrate that some people are more susceptible to caffeine intoxication.

There are a number of reasons for this susceptibility, such as having an underlying heart condition. But in Jackson's case, the most likely culprit was his liver.

Caffeine (and the related stimulants from tea and coca, theophyline and theobromine) is broken down in the liver by a specific enzyme (cytochrome P450 1A2 for the technical minded). Not everyone has the same amount of this enzyme in their livers for many reasons, such as the gene for the enzyme being missing or defective.

The reason you don't give chocolate to dogs is that they have very low levels of their version of the human enzyme, and are more susceptible to toxicity from theobromine and caffeine in chocolate.

Around 40% of Caucasians have a version of the enzyme that breaks down caffeine slowly. In these people, caffeine consumption is correlated with higher incidences of heart attack and high blood pressure.

But in this case, the reason was not a genetic variation but disease. The deceased had cirrhosis of the liver, which, among other things, greatly reduces the ability of the liver to break down a variety of chemicals, including caffeine.

Better Information

Jackson reportedly had 155 milligrams of caffeine per litre of his blood. But from the amount of caffeine he consumed, one would expect a blood level of somewhere between ten and 20 milligrams per litre, which is below the 80 milligrams per litre that's reportedly toxic.

The mints in question have a label warning on the back of the tin saying they contain high levels of caffeine, and advise against eating more than five in a 24-hour period (but its website doesn't have any warnings). The labels also warn caffeine-sensitive individuals against consuming them.

But most people with cirrhosis or hepatitis are not necessarily sensitive to caffeine, and so may not be aware that the warning applies to them. That is, if they read the back of the tin; the front of the tin makes no mention of caffeine at all, and consumers may not be aware they are eating caffeine-laced sweets.

There is, I think, a good case for more prominent labelling of caffeine-containing food stuffs and beverages, along with rewording of the warnings so they are clearer about who is at risk.

While death from caffeine overdose is fortunately very rare, this tragic case shows that there's more we can do to make it rarer still.

3

Caffeine Is a Drug

Murray Carpenter

Murray Carpenter is a journalist and author of Caffeinated: How Our Daily Habit Helps, Hurts and Hooks Us.

Caffeine is a difficult drug to understand. The amount of caffeine in a cup of coffee can vary greatly, even when purchased from the same source, from day to day. Although it is not regulated as a drug, caffeine acts like one and has the effects of dependence, withdrawal, and health complications. With the rise in popularity of energy products, more caffeine deaths have been reported. As a result, regulators are taking another look at caffeine as an additive. While regulating caffeine could prove difficult, the new generation of highly caffeinated energy drinks is drawing more attention to the question of what should be done to protect people from over consumption.

Propped up on my desk before me, there is a vacuum-sealed bag of white powder. Chemists would recognise this substance as a methylated xanthine, composed of tiny crystalline structures. It is a drug, and I have been under its influence nearly every day for the past 25 years. It is caffeine, and in moderation it makes us feel good. But it is a drug whose strength is consistently underestimated. You'd need to down about 50 cups of coffee at once, or 200 cups of tea, to approach a lethal level of caffeination—but if you go straight for the powder, you can get a lot very quickly.

On 9 April 2010, 23-year-old Michael Bedford was at a party near his home in Mansfield [England]. He ate two spoonfuls of caffeine powder he'd bought online, and washed them down with an energy drink. He began slurring his words, then vomited, collapsed and died. It's likely he ingested more than 5g [grams] of caffeine. The coroner cited caffeine's "cardiotoxic effects" as the cause of death.

Caffeine Content

How much caffeine is the average person taking on daily? When someone asks about our caffeine habits, we tend to reply in terms of how many cups of coffee we drink. But this is a wildly inadequate measure. One 40ml [milliliter] cup of coffee—the size often used in studies of caffeine consumption—could have less than 60mg [milligrams] of caffeine, while one 450ml cup could have nearly 10 times as much, but both could be considered one cup of coffee.

It is not easy to know how much caffeine is in your daily cup of coffee.

In an effort to make this easier, I came up with a measure called a Standard Caffeine Dose, or Scad. A Scad is 75mg. This is roughly equal to a shot of espresso, 150ml of coffee, a 250ml can of Red Bull, two 350ml cans of Coke or Pepsi, or a pint of Diet Coke. I take about four or five Scads daily. On a two-Scad day, I will feel slow; on a seven-Scad day, jittery.

Anyone will tell you that the British have remained allied with tea, not coffee, but that is only partly true. While the British still drink more tea, by volume, than coffee, they now get more of their caffeine from coffee than from tea. Surprisingly, colas and energy drinks now contribute nearly as much caffeine to the British diet as tea: 34mg daily versus 36mg daily.

It is not easy to know how much caffeine is in your daily cup of coffee. Forensic toxicologist Bruce Goldberger used to work in Baltimore [Maryland], identifying lethal drugs in the blood of overdose victims. But he turned his mind to a question with broader appeal: how much caffeine are we getting in our beverages? He and his colleagues analysed the contents of coffee drinks, publishing the results in 2003. They found huge caffeine differences not only between coffee brands but also between coffees from the same shop. He bought a 480ml cup of coffee from one branch of Starbucks on six consecutive days. Each time, he ordered the Breakfast Blend. The cup with the least caffeine had 260mg. One had twice that amount. Yet another clocked in at a whopping 564mg.

For a study published in 2012, Scottish researcher Thomas Crozier and his colleagues bought 20 espressos in Glasgow cafes. They found that the caffeine concentration varied from 56mg to 196mg per 28ml, with four cafes serving up espressos containing more than 200mg of caffeine.

Crozier and Goldberger's studies help to answer a question that many coffee drinkers have asked: why is it that on some days one cup of coffee puts you in absolute equipoise—brilliant but steady, relaxed but energetic—while other days it is not even enough to prop open your eyelids? And on other occasions, that very same cup, from the same cafe, will send you to the moon, jittery and anxious, your heart skittering? It is because the caffeine levels in coffee vary dramatically, depending on the natural growing conditions, the variety of coffee plant and the brewing strength.

Caffeine Dependence

Roland Griffiths is a prolific drug researcher. "I'm a psychopharmacologist, so I'm interested in the mood-altering effects of drugs," he says. "Caffeine to me is maybe the most fascinating compound, because it clearly is psychoactive, yet it is completely culturally accepted worldwide, or almost worldwide." While we talk, he sips caffeine-free Diet Coke from a mug bearing the structural diagram of the caffeine molecule.

Even though caffeine is not considered to be a drug of abuse, it has all the features of one, Griffiths says. "That is, it alters mood, it produces physical dependence and withdrawal upon abstinence, and some proportion of the population becomes dependent on it."

When Griffiths started his experiments on caffeine, he was a heavy user: "I think my consumption was probably 500–600mg a day, maybe higher." That's more than one litre of good coffee. When he decided to study caffeine withdrawal, he did it the hard way, personally going from a daily dose of seven Scads down to zero, and paying close attention to the havoc it wreaked on his body and brain. Did he go cold turkey? "No, no! I'm enough of a psychopharmacologist to know that's not how I would want to do it. I tapered back."

As part of a series of studies, using themselves as guinea pigs, Griffiths and his colleagues went on a steady daily dose of 100mg of caffeine. In one experiment, their caffeine was cut altogether for 12 days. Four of the seven subjects experienced symptoms including headaches, lethargy and an inability to concentrate. In the second phase, the researchers, still on a steady 100mg daily dose, went for single days without caffeine, separated by more than a week. In this case, "each of the seven subjects demonstrated a statistically significant withdrawal effect".

These scientists were not withdrawing from massive doses of caffeine, just the amount in about 150–240ml of coffee, a Scad and a third. That is all it takes to get hooked.

Coca-Cola owes its success to caffeine. Its early formulation had 80mg of caffeine per 250ml serving, and it was marketed as a pick-me-up. That was in 1909, when the US federal government first tried and failed to corral the emerging caffeine economy, leaving a vacuum that persists to this day. The American Food and Drug Administration (FDA) has long practised a dual regulatory role for caffeine, regulating it when it's packaged as an over-the-counter medication and mostly ignoring it when it is blended into drinks or labelled as a dietary supplement. But the new generation of energy products seems to have caught their attention.

Regulating Caffeine

When you crack open a can of Monster Energy, you first hear the hiss of the escaping carbonation. Poured into a glass, Monster is about the colour of a pale ale. On the tongue, well, it's an acquired taste: slightly metallic, syrupy sweet, a faint hint of orange and cream. No, it's not a hot cup of Colombian, but you could get used to it. Millions have. With a striking logo of three neon green claw marks and the slogan "Unleash the beast", Monster seems to be everywhere. In 2011, it surpassed Red Bull in US energy drink sales, by volume, according to *Beverage Digest*.

[The FDA] advised that people should consult their doctor before consuming energy drinks or shots. This seemed notable—dramatic, even.

Monster evolved from a product called Hansen's Energy, introduced by the juice company Hansen's Natural in 1997. Sales took off in 2002 when they came up with the Monster name, its memorable slogan and distinctive logo. (The claw-mark logo is now a popular tattoo, even among high school students.) Hansen's made its Monster cans twice the size of a Red Bull, but charged the same price. They developed a marketing strategy like those of other energy drinks, targeting young males with an energetic blend of heavy metal bands, action sports festivals and bikini models. Within seven years, it was a billion-dollar brand, with sales of nearly $2.4bn in 2012.

In the summer of that year, New York state attorney general Eric Schneiderman started to look at the marketing and advertising practices of companies who make energy drinks. Meanwhile, several US senators were putting pressure on the FDA to better regulate the industry. In August [2012], FDA assistant commissioner for legislation Jeanne Ireland responded to the senators' concerns with a five-page letter outlining the regulatory framework for energy drinks. She also discussed a death that was getting some attention.

Anais Fournier, a 14-year-old from Hagerstown, Maryland, drank a can of Monster on 16 December 2011. The next evening, with her friends at the Valley Mall, she drank another can of Monster Energy, bought from a sweet shop. Each can contained 240mg of caffeine (three Scads). A few hours after leaving the mall, Fournier was at home watching a movie with her family when she went into cardiac arrest and fell unconscious. At the hospital, doctors put her into a medically induced coma. Six days later, she was taken off life support and died. The coroner listed the cause of death as "cardiac arrhythmia due to caffeine toxicity complicating mitral valve regulation in the setting of Ehlers-Danlos syndrome" (a pre-existing medical condition).

In November 2012, the FDA released a comprehensive list of nearly eight years of what they call "adverse event reports" (consumer complaints) related to Monster, Rockstar and 5-Hour Energy products. It was a list of 93 events, including 13 deaths. There is no way of knowing whether the energy products caused the deaths, but it was enough to scare the public and prompt the FDA to announce an investigation. They advised that people should consult their doctor before consuming energy drinks or shots. This seemed notable— dramatic, even—particularly considering the fact that the agency does not recommend checking with GPs [general practitioners] before drinking colas or coffee.

Potential Health Problems

It is hard to unravel the health problems attributed to energy drinks. Any of us who use caffeine eventually take more than we want to and might experience the sensation of a pounding heart. A bit too much caffeine is unlikely to harm your heart. Even among those people with arrhythmias—disorders that cause the heart to beat too fast, too slowly or irregularly—caffeine does little harm. A 2011 literature review published in the *American Journal of Medicine* found no reason for concern. "It is understandable that most physicians are unsure of the advice they can provide about caffeine intake and arrhythmias," Daniel Pelchovitz and Jeffrey Goldberger wrote. "In most patients with known or suspected arrhythmia, caffeine in moderate doses is well tolerated and there is therefore no reason to restrict ingestion of caffeine." It would be easy to be sceptical of this finding: Goldberger is a consultant for Red Bull, and there is the sense that caffeine can feel hard on the heart. But, despite numerous studies, doctors have been unable to find a link between moderate caffeine use and heart disease or disturbance in most people. However, recent research does suggest an association between coffee and nonfatal heart attacks in people with a genetic predisposition to metabolise caffeine slowly.

It would be safe to assume that if a 240mg dose of caffeine, which Fournier consumed, could kill a person, then Starbucks would have seen at least a few deaths from its coffee, which might contain this amount of caffeine in a 350ml or 500ml cup. A person might drink energy drinks and then have a heart problem, but did the former cause the latter, or are they unrelated? It might be that people who suffer a heart attack after drinking an energy shot or energy drink are more likely to associate the heart trouble with the product than are people who suffer heart attacks after drinking coffee. It would be a simple explanation, and one that could hold some appeal for the energy drink industry. But in Fournier's case there was the coroner's report listing caffeine toxicity as the cause of death (although the coroner also mentioned a pre-existing medical condition).

On 17 October 2012, a team of attorneys filed a civil action with the Riverside County Superior Court of California. It was titled *Wendy Crossland and Richard Fournier; individually and as surviving parents of Anais Fournier v Monster Beverage Corporation*. The case contained seven complaints, including negligence and wrongful death. The lawyers sent out a press release, quoting Fournier's mother. "I was shocked to learn the FDA can regulate caffeine in a can of soda, but not these huge energy drinks," Wendy Crossland said. "These drinks are targeting teenagers with no oversight or accountability. [They] are death traps for young, developing girls and boys, like my daughter Anais."

The entire energy products industry, worth more than $10bn annually, has grown without the FDA's explicit approval.

Monster is defending the case. It is questioning the medical evidence and claims Fournier regularly drank energy drinks and Starbucks coffee. It says the autopsy report of caffeine toxicity was based only on Fournier's mother's report of her drinking an energy drink, not on a blood test. It has also detailed her heart conditions.

On 1 May 2013, a gaggle of food industry honchos from Wrigley, Mars [Wm. Wrigley Jr. Co. is owned by Mars Inc.] and legal and lobbying firm Patton Boggs, which represents the soft drink industry, rushed in to see Michael Taylor, the FDA's deputy commissioner for foods and veterinary medicine. On 29 April [2013], Taylor had announced the agency would be investigating the safety of adding caffeine to food products for the first time since 1980. Surprisingly, the item that finally spurred the FDA into action was not any of the more extreme energy products, but a gum.

In April [2013], Wrigley had introduced Alert Energy Caffeine Gum. But a week after the delegation met with the FDA, on 8 May [2013], Wrigley said it was pulling the product from the market. "After discussions with the FDA, we have a greater appreciation for its concern about the proliferation of caffeine in the nation's food supply," Wrigley announced. "We have paused the production, sales and marketing of Alert."

Energy Products and Regulation

A month later, I went to Maryland to interview Taylor. He told me that the new energy products have broken out of the typical boundaries around caffeine and are a far cry from coffee, tea and chocolate. And in the process, the food industry is skirting food additive regulations. Taylor drinks coffee and Diet Coke (sometimes caffeine-free), and understands the challenge of regulating caffeine and the limits regulators might face. "I got asked by somebody, 'Are we going to put age limits on coffee, so if you go to Starbucks, would you have to show ID?' I would consider that not realistic," he said. But he made a distinction between the more traditional uses of caffeine and the new breed of energy drinks. Holding a can of Monster, he said, "This is not a historic, cultural aspect of caffeine . . . What I found disturbing on this front was that in no case did the companies that are making these decisions come to us . . . and subject themselves to the scrutiny that would come." The entire energy products industry, worth more than $10bn annually, has grown without the FDA's explicit approval.

The UK [United Kingdom] is moving ahead of the US in caffeine labelling. Starting in December [2014], the Food Standards Agency will require new labels for energy drinks. Any drinks with caffeine concentrations higher than 150mg per litre must carry this label: "High caffeine content. Not recommended for children or pregnant or breastfeeding women."

The label must be placed in the same field of vision as the name of the energy drink and show the quantity of caffeine. It will appear on Red Bull, for example, with its concentration of 320mg per litre, but not Coca-Cola, with a lower concentration of 95mg per litre. In November last year, meanwhile, Morrisons became the first UK supermarket chain to ban sales of high-caffeine energy drinks to children.

Walking out of FDA headquarters, I passed a display case of the agency's notable efforts. There were packages of the drug thalidomide. There were a few patent medicines. The only caffeine was in a bottle of Formula One, an ephedra-caffeine blend that has been linked with heart trouble. (Supplements containing ephedra were banned and Formula One was reformulated.) I wondered what the case might hold in 20 years. Maybe some example of caffeinated excess now on the market—or, more likely, one that has yet to be formulated.

Travelling back to Maine that afternoon, I stopped for petrol. The counter next to the cash register was cluttered with energy shots and energy strips. And there, tucked into the front of the display tray, was a single pack of the Wrigley Alert Energy gum. It was the first I'd seen of the product Wrigley had tried to pull off the shelves. Of course, I bought it. Who knows? It might be worth something some day.

4

Caffeine Is Addictive

Addiction.com

Addiction.com is an online community for those affected by addiction. It is owned and operated by Elements Behavioral Health, a provider of treatment for addiction and mental health issues.

Caffeine withdrawal was added to the Diagnostic and Statistical Manual of Mental Disorders *in 2013 along with other caffeine-related disorders. Abruptly stopping caffeine consumption can trigger negative physical effects and mental and emotional disturbances. These symptoms qualify caffeine as an addictive substance and its withdrawal as a mental health concern.*

Caffeine-related disorders are a group of conditions that revolve in some way around the use of coffee or other caffeine-containing substances.

The American Psychiatric Association lists these disorders as mental health issues in its *Diagnostic and Statistical Manual of Mental Disorders* (DSM), which functions as an everyday guide for identifying and categorizing psychological/psychiatric symptoms. One caffeine-related condition, called caffeine withdrawal, appears for the first time in the 5th edition of the DSM, released in 2013. Another condition—called caffeine use disorder—does not qualify as a diagnosable problem, but is still listed in DSM 5 in a category designated for future research.

Caffeine-Related Disorder Basics

DSM 5 contains four officially recognized caffeine-related diagnoses: caffeine intoxication, caffeine withdrawal, "other" caffeine-induced disorders and "unspecified" caffeine-related disorder.

In turn, all caffeine-related disorders belong to a group of conditions known as substance-related disorders. Only one of the caffeine-related disorders, caffeine intoxication, appeared in the previous edition of the DSM.

The "other" caffeine-induced disorders listing replaces two more specific listings in DSM IV, called caffeine-induced sleep disorder and caffeine-induced anxiety disorder. "Unspecified" caffeine-related disorder replaces a condition in DSM IV known as caffeine-related disorder not otherwise specified.

In order to qualify for a caffeine intoxication diagnosis, the affected individual must experience substantial life disruption or mental distress as a result of his or her condition.

Caffeine withdrawal was included in DSM 5 in response to research findings regarding the potential impact of an abrupt cessation or decrease in regular caffeine usage.

Caffeine Intoxication and Other Disorders

The definition for caffeine intoxication in DSM 5 is the same as the definition for caffeine intoxication listed in DSM IV. People affected by this disorder are typically under the influence of more than 250 mg of caffeine (equivalent to more than 16–24 oz of coffee).

They also have a minimum of five physical and mental symptoms that stem from caffeine's effects. The potential symptoms include:

- Unusual twitching of the muscles

- Unusual excitability

- Intestinal upset

- Heightened urine output

- An abnormally nervous disposition

- An abnormally restless disposition

- Facial redness

- Sleeplessness

- An accelerated or irregular heartbeat

- Unusually high energy reserves

- Disjointed speech or thought

- The presence of aimless, uncontrolled body movements.

In order to qualify for a caffeine intoxication diagnosis, the affected individual must experience substantial life disruption or mental distress as a result of his or her condition.

He or she must also lack other physical or mental problems that explain the symptoms in effect.

Before it can qualify as a mental health concern, caffeine withdrawal (and all other forms of substance withdrawal) must meet certain criteria listed in the DSM.

The first of these criteria states that the negative effects of stopping or reducing substance intake must appear in long-term, heavy users of that substance.

The second criterion states that the unpleasant feelings associated with withdrawal must cause meaningful mental anguish or disrupt some key aspect of everyday life.

The third withdrawal criterion states that the affected individual's symptoms must not stem from some other psychological or physical issue.

Caffeine withdrawal was given official status as a mental health problem in DSM 5 because current findings indicate that it meets all three of these criteria in at least some circumstances.

The "other" caffeine-induced disorders diagnosis was created out of recognition of the fact that caffeine use can potentially trigger other mental health concerns apart from sleep-related problems or anxiety.

When making a diagnosis, doctors must identify the specific caffeine-related conditions present in their patients.

The "unspecified" caffeine-related disorder diagnosis is designed to address caffeine-related mental health problems that don't fit well within the definitions of any of the other caffeine-related disorders.

Some of the substances listed in the DSM are subject to abuse by their users, and can also produce some form of psychological or physical dependence.

In previous editions of the DSM, abuse-related problems and dependence-related problems were listed separately for each substance (e.g., cocaine abuse and cocaine dependence, or alcohol abuse and alcohol dependence). However, current scientific knowledge does not support the interpretation of abuse and dependence as strictly distinct issues; rather, abuse- and dependence-related issues typically overlap with some degree of unpredictability. In recognition of this reality, DSM 5 does not allow the separate diagnosis of abuse or dependence.

Instead, it allows the diagnosis of various substance use disorders, which include symptoms once split between substance abuse and substance dependence.

Some doctors believe that, in at least certain cases, caffeine intake can lead to the onset of problems that merit a diagnosis of caffeine use disorder. However, not all doctors agree with this position, and caffeine use disorder is not a diagnosable condition in DSM 5.

Instead, this disorder is listed in a portion of DSM 5—called Section III—reserved for unofficial conditions that are well defined enough to warrant more research and conceptual exploration. At some point in the future, the American Psychiatric Association will decide whether to include caffeine use disorder with the officially designated caffeine-related disorders or remove it entirely from the *Diagnostic and Statistical Manual.*

5

Caffeine Improves Cognitive Performance

Institute for Scientific Information on Coffee

The Institute for Scientific Information on Coffee is a nonprofit organization devoted to the study and disclosure of the science related to coffee and health.

Caffeine use has been shown through multiple studies to improve visual attention, help sustain focus, and improve reaction time. Additionally, research has demonstrated that caffeine can reduce work accidents and is as effective as a nap for maintaining alertness during evening driving. Although too much caffeine can reduce it, working memory can also be improved with caffeine consumption. Likewise, moderate amounts of caffeine can reduce anxiety, while higher doses can increase anxiety. Moderate caffeine use is key to improving cognitive performance.

It is well-recognised that coffee drinking contributes to increased wakefulness and alertness. Most of the work on coffee consumption and mental performance focuses on caffeine.

Caffeine is known to have a mild stimulant effect. Research has been conducted for many years to investigate the positive role of caffeinated coffee on improved attention, alertness, reaction time and memory.

In 2011 the European Food Safety Authority (EFSA) evaluated a substantial amount of studies on the effects of caffeine on mental performance, and concluded that there is sufficient scientific evidence to support a cause and effect relationship for the effect of caffeine on alertness and attention.

Caffeine and Visual Attention

Numerous studies have investigated the effects of caffeine ingestion on visual attention. EFSA evaluated a significant number of studies and concluded that caffeine increases both selective attention (focussing on the relevant stimulus) and sustained attention (maintaining focused attention over an extended period of time). A 75mg [milligram] serving of caffeine, the amount found in around one regular cup of coffee, has been demonstrated to increase attention. Higher caffeine intakes, such as those found in more than one or two cups of coffee, do not necessarily result in additional increases in alertness. It is thought that the relationship between the level of arousal and task performance follows an inverted U-curve i.e. performance decrements can occur due to both under- and over-arousal. A review published in 2012 suggests that caffeine improves performance on both simple and complex attention tasks, concluding that caffeine has clear beneficial effects on attention, and that these effects are even more widespread than previously assumed.

In 2010, in a series of experiments by the same research group, the effects of caffeine on attention were compared in non-habitual and habitual caffeine consumers. In non-habitual caffeine consumers, the effects were dose-dependent and the best results for visual attention were achieved with 200mg of caffeine (the equivalent of around two cups of coffee). In habitual consumers, the amount required to enhance both vigilance and visual attention was higher, i.e. 400mg (around four cups of coffee). In the same manner, caffeine enhanced real-world language processing and improved the rate of detecting errors in discourse. As in the previous studies low-caffeine consumers had the highest rates of improvements with 200mg of caffeine while high consumers' rates peaked with 400mg.

The expectation of having consumed caffeine can also affect attention and psychomotor speed. These findings are in agreement with those of an older imaging study, reporting that caffeine and expectation of caffeine activate the same brain areas, but in a more limited way in the latter case. At this point the underlying psychological mechanisms of these responses are not clear.

The effects of caffeine on alertness are most often clearest in situations where an individual's alertness level is reduced.

Caffeine and Reaction Time

The positive effects of caffeine on reaction time have been studied extensively over the last decades. An overview of the studies can be found in the EFSA evaluation.

Other experiments have confirmed the positive effect of caffeine on reaction time, while 'time perception' (the sense of time passing in an individual) and 'time production' (the time it takes to produce something following a stimulus) appear relatively insensitive to caffeine. Thus, it appears that interval timing and reaction time performance are not always necessarily interdependent.

Caffeine, Alertness and Safety in Daily-Life Situations

The effects of caffeine on alertness are most often clearest in situations where an individual's alertness level is reduced, such as when they are suffering from the common cold, the post-lunch dip or working at night.

• During night work, caffeine has also been shown to reduce cognitive failures and accidents by about half in subjects consuming over 220mg caffeine daily, i.e. the amount found in approximately two cups of coffee.

• Moreover, caffeine reduces cognitive failures in the non-working population.

• The latter two studies point to the benefits of caffeine consumption on performance and safety.

Caffeine is often consumed at awakening to increase alertness and fight sleep inertia.

• Sleep inertia is characterised by a decline in motor dexterity and a subjective feeling of grogginess immediately following an abrupt awakening. The impaired alertness may interfere with the ability to perform mental or physical tasks. Sleep inertia can also refer to the tendency of a person wanting to return to sleep.

• Caffeine has been shown to overcome sleep inertia, which may explain, in part, the popularity of caffeine-containing beverages after waking up.

Finally, the efficacy of coffee versus napping on night time highway driving has been compared.

• It appears that drinking one strong coffee (125ml containing 200mg caffeine) is as effective as a 30 minute nap to reduce driving impairment without altering subsequent sleep.

• A 2012 study found that subjective driving quality during a simulated two hour monotonous highway driving test was significantly improved in the first hour after consuming a single cup of caffeinated coffee (80mg of caffeine).

• Likewise, another study reported that a 30 minute break including a short nap (less than 15 minutes), or a coffee containing 150–200mg caffeine, were very effective. This effect was even more prominent when the two were combined. This amount of caffeine also resulted in reduced driving incidents in a simulated driving test, in the early morning for 30 minutes following no sleep, or about two hours after sleep restriction.

• A case-control study showed caffeinated beverages, such as coffee, to be associated with a reduced risk of crashing for long distance, commercial motor vehicle drivers.

• In addition, slow-release caffeine (300mg) has also been reported to reduce lane drifting, speed deviation and accident liability in a simulated driving test.

These data suggest that caffeine can serve as an effective countermeasure to the performance decrements induced by sleep-deprivation, particularly when there is no opportunity to take a nap.

However, it must be noted that, while caffeine (200–400mg, i.e. the equivalent of 2–4 cups of coffee) may increase alertness and reduce reaction time after alcohol ingestion, alcohol-induced impairment will not be counteracted by caffeine in drivers. . . .

Caffeine and Memory

Beneficial effects of caffeine intake on improving working memory have been reported. Low doses of caffeine enhance working memory performance, while higher doses are found to decrease it, possibly due to over-stimulation.

• Comparable results have been shown in low-load memory tasks versus high-load memory tasks. Caffeine has been shown to have beneficial effects on performance in both low-difficulty and low-load memory tasks. High-load and complicated tasks induced increased arousal by themselves; so in these tasks, caffeine could lead to over-arousal. Thus caffeine appears to improve working memory performance under conditions that otherwise produce low arousal states.

• A 2010 study suggested such an effect may be linked to personality. Caffeine improved working memory performance in extroverts but not in introverts. Further research in this area would be of interest.

• Another study tested college students to see if they could recall words from six different lists comprising 15 words each, after 200mg caffeine administration (the equivalent of two cups of coffee). The words on each list were semantically related to a single word (a "critical lure") that was not present in the list. The students recalled more listed words and more "critical lures" with caffeine intake than with the placebo. Caffeine appeared to intensify the connections among listed words and critical lures, hence enhancing both true and false memory. [True memory—participants memorised and recalled only words from the list; false memory—participants quoted words that were not on the original list but were related to the list words, i.e. induced by the lure.]

Low to moderate doses of caffeine (around two to five cups of coffee per day) improve hedonic tone and reduce anxiety.

Synergistic Effects of Caffeine and Glucose

Caffeine and glucose absorbed together have beneficial synergistic effects on sustained attention and verbal memory.

Combined administration of glucose and caffeine modulates neural activity in a network involving the parietal and prefrontal cortex related to sustained attention. Synergistic consumption of both substances is thought to increase the efficiency of the attentional system, as subjects who received the combined beverage had similar performance to the other subjects, but required less activation of attentional brain areas.

Further studies using larger samples and different levels of caffeine, glucose and cognitive effort will be necessary to better understand the combined effects of both substances.

Caffeine and Mood

It is well-known that low to moderate doses of caffeine (around two to five cups of coffee per day) improve hedonic tone and reduce anxiety. Whereas high doses can increase tense arousal, including anxiety, nervousness, and jitteriness.

A dose-related improvement in subjective measures of calmness and interest are found after caffeine, suggesting that mood improvement may depend on baseline arousal.

• Older adults are more sensitive than younger individuals to the mood-enhancing effects of caffeine, and mood effects are also influenced by the time of the day, with the most prominent effects showing in the late morning.

• Moreover, mood is not only modulated by caffeine itself but also by the expectation of having consumed caffeine, which improves mood together with attention.

• Caffeine tends to benefit habitual consumers' (compared to non-consumers) mood more, but there are greater improvements in performance when taken by non-consumers.

• Using the well-accepted Profile of Mood States (POMS) self-rating scale and the Bakan test for cognitive performance, a 2009 double-blind study concluded that a moderate dose of caffeine (200mg—the equivalent of two regular cups of coffee), together with a low carbohydrate intake (50g white bread) positively influenced mood and cognitive performance, while carbohydrate alone did not. This indicates that, in the caffeine/carbohydrate combination group, the key element leading to improved mood and mental performance was the presence of caffeine.

• A study investigating the role of caffeine on social support asked participants who received either caffeinated coffee (150mg caffeine), or decaffeinated coffee (9mg caffeine), to imagine a fictitious person and to play the Mixed Motive Game with that person 45 minutes after coffee consumption. Caffeinated coffee increased co-operative game behaviour and sadness communication, suggesting that caffeinated coffee may improve social support and relieve depressive symptoms.

• A study of 50,739 women (average age 63 years), part of the Nurses' Health Study, looked at caffeine and depression. It appeared that women who consumed 2–3 or at least 4 cups of caffeinated coffee per day were 15% or 20% less likely to develop depression, respectively, compared to those who drank at most one cup of caffeinated coffee per week. The consumption of decaffeinated coffee had no impact on depression risk.

This observational study suggests the possibility of a protective effect of caffeine on depression risk.

• Another cohort study of Finnish men, reported a 77% risk reduction for depression in heavy coffee drinkers (those who consumed over 813mg caffeine daily, around eight cups of coffee). This effect was limited to coffee and was not found with either tea or caffeine alone.

• A 2013 Japanese cross-sectional study reviewed the impact of consumption of both green tea and coffee on depressive symptoms, suggesting that both green tea (more than four cups per day) and coffee (more than two cups per day) may offer protection against depression.

• A small pilot study reported that caffeinated coffee had a more robust positive effect on high-level mood and attention processes than decaffeinated coffee. Interestingly, the authors found that decaffeinated coffee, which is rich in antioxidants such as chlorogenic acids, could also improve mood and performance. This suggests that substances other than caffeine, like chlorogenic acids, may also affect mood and performance. However this effect needs to be confirmed in a larger group of individuals.

• Finally, coffee and caffeine consumption might be favoured by some specific patient groups, including patients with bipolar disorders who were reported to consume more social drugs such as tobacco and coffee than the general population, and schizophrenic patients. It has been hypothesized that patients smoke and drink coffee to reduce medication side effects like anhedonia or improve cognitive symptoms linked to the treatment.

6

Caffeine Does Not Improve Cognitive Performance

Travis Bradberry

Travis Bradberry is the coauthor of Emotional Intelligence 2.0 *and* Leadership 2.0 *and a frequent contributor of articles on the subject of emotional intelligence and performance.*

Many studies suggest caffeine enhances cognitive performance. However, reducing or ideally eliminating caffeine is a much more effective method to improve performance. As caffeine is addictive, the benefits seen in studies are actually due to the cessation of caffeine withdrawal symptoms, not to the caffeine itself. Caffeine is also responsible for increasing adrenaline in the body, which can increase anxiety and interfere with sleep. To truly improve cognitive performance, it would be far better to completely eliminate caffeine from the diet.

This week's tip for improving your performance is the most simple and straightforward method I've provided thus far. For many people, this tip has the potential to have a bigger impact than any other single action. The catch? You have to cut down on caffeine, and as any caffeine drinker can attest, this is easier said than done.

For those who aren't aware, the ability to manage your emotions and remain calm under pressure has a direct link to your performance. TalentSmart has conducted research with more than a million people, and we've found that 90 percent

Travis Bradberry, "Caffeine: The Silent Killer of Success," *Inc.*, February 3, 2015. Inc.com. © 2015 Inc. Magazine. All rights reserved. Reproduced by permission.

of top performers are high in emotional intelligence. These individuals are skilled at managing their emotions (even in times of high stress) in order to remain calm and in control.

The Good: Isn't Really Good

Most people start drinking caffeine because it makes them feel more alert and improves their mood. Many studies suggest that caffeine actually improves cognitive task performance (memory, attention span, etc.) in the short-term. Unfortunately, these studies fail to consider the participants' caffeine habits. New research from Johns Hopkins [University] Medical School shows that performance increases due to caffeine intake are the result of caffeine drinkers experiencing a short-term reversal of caffeine withdrawal. By controlling for caffeine use in study participants, John Hopkins researchers found that caffeine-related performance improvement is non-existent without caffeine withdrawal. In essence, coming off caffeine reduces your cognitive performance and has a negative impact on your mood. The only way to get back to normal is to drink caffeine, and when you do drink it, you feel like it's taking you to new heights. In reality, the caffeine is just taking your performance back to normal for a short period.

The Bad: Adrenaline

Drinking caffeine triggers the release of adrenaline. Adrenaline is the source of the fight-or-flight response, a survival mechanism that forces you to stand up and fight or run for the hills when faced with a threat. The fight-or-flight mechanism sidesteps rational thinking in favor of a faster response. This is great when a bear is chasing you, but not so great when you're responding to a curt email. When caffeine puts your brain and body into this hyper-aroused state, your emotions overrun your behavior.

Irritability and anxiety are the most commonly seen emotional effects of caffeine, but caffeine enables all of your emotions to take charge.

You can ... improve the quality of your sleep by reducing your caffeine intake.

The negative effects of a caffeine-generated adrenaline surge are not just behavioral. Researchers at Carnegie Mellon University found that large doses of caffeine raise blood pressure, stimulate the heart, and produce rapid shallow breathing, which readers of *Emotional Intelligence 2.0* know deprives the brain of the oxygen needed to keep your thinking calm and rational.

The Ugly: Sleep

When you sleep, your brain literally recharges, shuffling through the day's memories and storing or discarding them (which causes dreams), so that you wake up alert and clear-headed. Your self-control, focus, memory, and information-processing speed are all reduced when you don't get enough—or the right kind—of sleep. Your brain is very fickle when it comes to sleep. For you to wake up feeling rested, your brain needs to move through an elaborate series of cycles. You can help this process along and improve the quality of your sleep by reducing your caffeine intake.

Here's why you'll want to: caffeine has a six-hour half-life, which means it takes a full twenty-four hours to work its way out of your system. Have a cup of joe at 8 a.m., and you'll still have 25 percent of the caffeine in your body at 8 p.m. Anything you drink after noon will still be at 50 percent strength at bedtime. Any caffeine in your bloodstream—with the negative effects increasing with the dose—makes it harder to fall asleep.

When you do finally fall asleep, the worst is yet to come. Caffeine disrupts the quality of your sleep by reducing rapid eye movement (REM) sleep, the deep sleep when your body recuperates and processes emotions. When caffeine disrupts your sleep, you wake up the next day with an emotional handicap. You're naturally going to be inclined to grab a cup of coffee or an energy drink to try to make yourself feel better. The caffeine produces surges of adrenaline, which adds to your emotional handicap. Caffeine and lack of sleep leave you feeling tired in the afternoon, so you drink more caffeine, which leaves even more of it in your bloodstream at bedtime. Caffeine very quickly creates a vicious cycle.

Like any stimulant, caffeine is physiologically and psychologically addictive. If you do choose to lower your caffeine intake, you should do so slowly under the guidance of a qualified medical professional. The researchers at Johns Hopkins found that caffeine withdrawal causes headache, fatigue, sleepiness, and difficulty concentrating. Some people report feeling flulike symptoms, depression, and anxiety after reducing intake by as little as one cup a day. Slowly tapering your caffeine dosage each day can greatly reduce these withdrawal symptoms.

7

Caffeine May Delay the Onset of Alzheimer's Disease

Advanced Healthcare Network

Advanced Healthcare Network publishes a series of free news-magazines designed to enhance the lives of healthcare professionals.

A study from the University of South Florida suggests caffeine delays the onset of Alzheimer's disease and may reduce the risk of developing the disease altogether. Further, caffeine consumption throughout adulthood has other protective cognitive benefits. Since caffeine consumed through coffee appears to have the most benefit, a yet-unidentified component of coffee combined with caffeine appears to provide optimal benefit. Caffeine through coffee consumption could improve the quality of life for millions of people.

Those cups of coffee that you drink every day to keep alert appear to have an extra perk—especially if you're an older adult. A recent study monitoring the memory and thinking processes of people older than 65 found that all those with higher blood caffeine levels avoided the onset of Alzheimer's disease in the two-to-four years of study follow-up. Moreover, coffee appeared to be the major or only source of caffeine for these individuals.

Researchers from the University of South Florida [USF] and the University of Miami say the case control study provides the first direct evidence that caffeine/coffee intake is associated with a reduced risk of dementia or delayed onset. Their findings appeared in the online version of an article published in June [2012] in the *Journal of Alzheimer's Disease*. The collaborative study involved 124 people, ages 65 to 86, in Tampa and Miami [Florida].

"These intriguing results suggest that older adults with mild memory impairment who drink moderate levels of coffee—about 3 cups a day—will not convert to Alzheimer's disease—or at least will experience a substantial delay before converting to Alzheimer's," said study lead author Dr. Chuanhai Cao, a neuroscientist at the USF College of Pharmacy and the USF Health Byrd Alzheimer's Institute. "The results from this study, along with our earlier studies in Alzheimer's mice, are very consistent in indicating that moderate daily caffeine/coffee intake throughout adulthood should appreciably protect against Alzheimer's disease later in life."

Protection Against Cognitive Impairment

The study shows this protection probably occurs even in older people with early signs of the disease, called mild cognitive impairment, or MCI. Patients with MCI already experience some short-term memory loss and initial Alzheimer's pathology in their brains. Each year, about 15 percent of MCI patients progress to full-blown Alzheimer's disease. The researchers focused on study participants with MCI, because many were destined to develop Alzheimer's within a few years.

Caffeinated coffee appeared to be the main, if not exclusive, source of caffeine in the memory-protected MCI [mild cognitive impairment] patients.

Blood caffeine levels at the study's onset were substantially lower (51 percent less) in participants diagnosed with MCI who progressed to dementia during the two-to-four year follow-up than in those whose mild cognitive impairment remained stable over the same period.

No one with MCI who later developed Alzheimer's had initial blood caffeine levels above a critical level of 1200 ng/ml [nanograms per milliliter]—equivalent to drinking several cups of coffee a few hours before the blood sample was drawn. In contrast, many with stable MCI had blood caffeine levels higher than this critical level.

"We found that 100 percent of the MCI patients with plasma caffeine levels above the critical level experienced no conversion to Alzheimer's disease during the two-to-four year follow-up period," said study co-author Dr. Gary Arendash.

The researchers believe higher blood caffeine levels indicate habitually higher caffeine intake, most probably through coffee. Caffeinated coffee appeared to be the main, if not exclusive, source of caffeine in the memory-protected MCI patients, because they had the same profile of blood immune markers as Alzheimer's mice given caffeinated coffee. Alzheimer's mice given caffeine alone or decaffeinated coffee had a very different immune marker profile.

Since 2006, Cao and Arendash have published several studies investigating the effects of caffeine/coffee administered to Alzheimer's mice. Most recently, they reported that caffeine interacts with a yet unidentified component of coffee to boost blood levels of a critical growth factor that seems to fight off the Alzheimer's disease process.

"We are not saying that moderate coffee consumption will completely protect people from Alzheimer's disease." Cao cautioned. "However, we firmly believe that moderate coffee consumption can appreciably reduce your risk of Alzheimer's or delay its onset."

Alzheimer's pathology is a process in which plaques and tangles accumulate in the brain, killing nerve cells, destroying neural connections, and ultimately leading to progressive and irreversible memory loss. Since the neurodegenerative disease starts one or two decades before cognitive decline becomes apparent, the study authors point out, any intervention to cut the risk of Alzheimer's should ideally begin that far in advance of symptoms.

Best Dietary Option?

"Moderate daily consumption of caffeinated coffee appears to be the best dietary option for long-term protection against Alzheimer's memory loss," Arendash said. "Coffee is inexpensive, readily available, easily gets into the brain, and has few side-effects for most of us. Moreover, our studies show that caffeine and coffee appear to directly attack the Alzheimer's disease process."

In addition to Alzheimer's disease, moderate caffeine/coffee intake appears to reduce the risk of several other diseases of aging, including Parkinson's disease, stroke, Type II diabetes, and breast cancer. However, supporting studies for these benefits have all been observational and controlled clinical trials are needed to definitively demonstrate therapeutic value.

A study tracking the health and coffee consumption of more than 400,000 older adults for 13 years, and published earlier this year in the *New England Journal of Medicine*, found that coffee drinkers reduced their risk of dying from heart disease, lung disease, pneumonia, stroke, diabetes, infections, and even injuries and accidents.

With new Alzheimer's diagnostic guidelines encompassing the full continuum of the disease, approximately 10 million Americans now fall within one of three developmental stages of Alzheimer's disease—Alzheimer's disease brain pathology only, MCI, or diagnosed Alzheimer's disease. That number is expected to climb even higher as the baby-boomer generation continues to enter older age, unless an effective and proven preventive measure is identified.

"If we could conduct a large cohort study to look into the mechanisms of how and why coffee and caffeine can delay or prevent Alzheimer's disease, it might result in billions of dollars in savings each year in addition to improved quality of life," Cao said.

8

Caffeine May Be Beneficial for the Treatment of ADHD

Jane Collingwood

Jane Collingwood is a mental health writer for the website Psych Central.

Anecdotal evidence and some scientific studies have shown promise for caffeine as a therapy for attention deficit hyperactivity disorder (ADHD) in both adults and children. However, overconsumption can be dangerous and habitual use may lesson the benefits. Despite the promise of caffeine in the treatment of ADHD, care should be taken when consuming the substance. Caffeine is a stimulant and can result in unwanted side effects, such as irritability, anxiety, and insomnia; its effectiveness is also reduced when used over a long period of time.

Attention deficit hyperactivity disorder (ADHD) is now one of the most common children's mental health conditions. It involves symptoms of inattention or impulsivity and hyperactivity that lead to behavioral impairments. Approximately 50 percent of children diagnosed with ADHD continue to show clinically significant symptoms and impairment as adults.

A great deal of research has investigated the possible role of caffeine in ADHD. Caffeine is a psychoactive stimulant drug, which can increase alertness and reduce drowsiness. Coffee, tea, soft drinks and chocolate all contain caffeine and are consumed around the world. Approximately 90 percent of adults in North America consume caffeine daily.

It is widely believed that caffeine boosts attention in normal adults, but research results are unclear. Some studies find better performance on memory tasks; others find that caffeine aids concentration but impairs short-term memory. There is also a general belief that caffeine makes people more anxious and hinders sleep. Caffeine withdrawal may trigger headache, fatigue, irritability and nervousness.

The effectiveness of coffee in calming ADHD children has become a great discussion point on websites and forums.

As it is a stimulant, caffeine has been investigated as a potential treatment for attention deficit disorder. Its use as a therapy is not widespread because it was found in research studies to be less efficient than other stimulants. But experts writing in 2008 suggest the doses were too low to have a consistent effect. They say that if caffeine proves useful, it "would represent a qualitative increment over the traditional repeated use of psychostimulants, which can have severe side effects if repeatedly used in children."

Caffeine's Effectiveness

Anecdotal evidence suggests that many individuals are already using caffeine to self-medicate ADHD in themselves or their children. Many sufferers find it has the opposite effect than it does in other people: instead of making them more active and stimulated, it actually has more of a "calm-down" effect, and encourages sleep.

The effectiveness of coffee in calming ADHD children has become a great discussion point on websites and forums. Many adults with ADHD also turn to coffee. In fact, some can't do without it; caffeine's stimulating effect helps them focus and stay on task.

A similar outcome has been found in animals. A 2005 study of rats with hyperactivity, impulsivity, poor attention, and deficits in learning and memory found a significant improvement in test results when caffeine was administered to the rats beforehand.

The researchers, from the Federal University of Santa Catarina in Brazil, explain that these rats are "considered to be a suitable genetic model for the study of ADHD, since they display hyperactivity, impulsivity, poorly sustained attention, and deficits in learning and memory processes."

The rats received a dose of caffeine 30 minutes before training, immediately after training, or 30 minutes before a test session in a water maze. These rats needed significantly more training sessions to learn the maze than ordinary rats, but then performed similarly in the test session 48 hours later.

Pre-training caffeine improved the learning deficit in the "ADHD" rats, but had no effect on the other rats. Caffeine given post-training made no difference to either group. "These results demonstrate a selective learning deficit which can be attenuated by pre-training administration of caffeine," say the researchers.

Caffeine certainly appears to be beneficial for some adults and children with ADHD. But just because it is easily accessible without a prescription, it is still a drug and this does not guarantee a lack of side effects. Overconsumption can be dangerous, especially when consumed on a regular basis over a long period of time. Consuming sugar alongside caffeine in coffee, tea, cola or chocolate may exacerbate attention deficit disorder symptoms.

What's more, the effects of caffeine are likely to be more short-lived than those from conventional medication, and may diminish over time, as habitual intake can lead to increased tolerance.

A condition known as *caffeinism* can be triggered when caffeine is consumed in large amounts over an extended period of time. Caffeinism causes nervousness, irritability, anxiety, tremulousness, muscle twitching, insomnia, headaches and heart palpitations. A high intake over time can also lead to peptic ulcers and other gastrointestinal problems.

Caffeine use for ADHD should always be discussed with a physician and may not preclude the need for other medication or therapy.

9

Health Check: Does Caffeine Enhance Performance?

Chris Forbes-Ewan

Chris Forbes-Ewan is senior nutritionist at the Defence Science and Technology Organization, part of Australia's Department of Defence.

The International Olympic Committee's ban on caffeine use by athletes was lifted in 2004. Caffeine, which can enhance athletic performance, can now be used freely even by elite athletes. Caffeine doesn't cause dehydration and careful dosing should avoid any adverse effects. For those looking to use caffeine for athletic training and performance, energy drinks provide the best source because, unlike coffee or tea, the amount of caffeine per serving is consistent. Caffeine is safe and effective for most athletes.

Unlike many drugs, caffeine may be taken legally by people of all ages, which helps make it the world's most widely used stimulant.

Approximately 80% of the world's caffeine is consumed in the form of coffee; it's been estimated that 500 billion cups of coffee are consumed throughout the world every year.

Tea, chocolate, cola drinks, and energy drinks and shots are the other main sources of caffeine.

Impact on Physical Performance

Caffeine has been used to good effect by athletes as an aid to physical performance for many years. Initially, it was believed to be of greatest benefit in endurance events (marathon running, for instance, or long-distance swimming).

More recently, we've realised that caffeine also boosts performance for short-term, high-intensity activities, such as middle-distance running, and stop-start sports, such as tennis.

Until a decade or so ago, it was thought that very high doses of caffeine (higher than could be obtained by simply drinking coffee, for example) were needed to enhance athletic performance.

Such high doses could usually only be obtained from caffeine-containing capsules, and often led to adverse side effects.

Consequently, the International Olympic Committee (IOC) banned caffeine use by athletes above a certain level of intake.

But by early this century, it became clear that moderate doses of caffeine—achievable by drinking coffee, tea or energy drinks—were just as effective as very high doses for enhancing physical performance. And they had minimal risk of side effects.

It was also discovered that caffeine intake is "self-limiting" to some extent, that is, extremely high doses are likely to have a detrimental effect on athletic performance.

A dose of about three milligrams of caffeine per kilogram of body weight will give you the desired boost to performance.

So, in 2004, the IOC ban on caffeine was completely lifted; Olympic athletes may now take as much caffeine as they like.

How Much Is Enough?

What, then, is the most appropriate source of caffeine if you're an athlete who wants to safely obtain a performance benefit?

Well, you could try coffee or tea, but the amount of caffeine in these beverages varies greatly. Energy drinks, on the other hand, are formulated to contain a known quantity of caffeine, so they allow for a more controlled intake.

A dose of about three milligrams of caffeine per kilogram of body weight will give you the desired boost to performance, with little likelihood of inducing the "caffeine shakes" that can result from overdosing.

So, for example, if an energy drink contains 80 milligrams of caffeine, and you weigh 55 kilograms, a couple of cans of energy drink will provide the recommended dose.

Some people believe that caffeine is a diuretic, that it promotes excessive urine production and therefore leads to dehydration. This is not correct, at least when caffeine is consumed in moderate amounts by habitual users.

People who regularly drink tea, coffee, cola drinks, energy drinks or energy shots can expect to receive the desired performance enhancement from caffeine without experiencing greater dehydration.

Making You Sharper

There's also evidence that caffeine improves some aspects of mental performance. Doses up to about 200 milligrams (similar to the dose that enhances physical performance) lead to increasingly quicker reactions, increased alertness, elevated mood and improvements in activities such as typing (greater typing speed with fewer mistakes).

The quantity of caffeine needed to enhance mental performance can be obtained by drinking one or two cups of coffee, one or two cans of energy drink, or several cups of tea. (But note the earlier advice that caffeine concentration is very variable in coffee and tea.)

People who need to maintain vigilance during a period when they would normally be asleep, such as long-distance truck drivers, nightwatchmen, shift workers, students "cramming" for exams and soldiers on sentry duty, often use caffeine from coffee, tea, energy drinks and shots or capsules to keep them awake and alert.

The US Army now uses a commercially available caffeinated chewing gum called "Stay Alert" in one of its combat rations (the First Strike Ration). This ration is issued to soldiers who are expected to take part in operations of up to 72 hours with minimal sleep. Stay Alert gum contains 100 milligrams of caffeine per stick and there are five sticks in the First Strike Ration.

A Little Doubt

In the interests of objectivity, I should point out that a small minority of researchers believe that caffeine does not truly enhance mental performance. Rather, they claim that taking caffeine will simply overcome the drop in performance that results from caffeine withdrawal in people who are used to having caffeine in their body.

But looking at data from military studies I'm familiar with, I believe there's little room for doubt that caffeine can greatly enhance at least some aspects of cognitive performance, particularly when people are sleep-deprived.

It's important to keep in mind though that overdosing on caffeine is potentially dangerous, particularly for those (mostly young) people who consume too many energy drinks or shots—especially if they combine these with alcohol.

Caffeine undoubtedly enhances many aspects of physical performance, and very likely several aspects of mental performance too. And unlike most performance-enhancing drugs, it's legal, readily available, and comes in forms that are highly acceptable to most people.

10

Are Olympic Athletes Legally Doping?

Cindy Kuzma

Cindy Kuzma is an independent health and fitness writer.

Some athletic organizations, including the National Collegiate Athletic Association, limit the use of caffeine supplements for sports performance. Caffeine use, however, is allowed in the Olympics despite the advantage it gives athletes and despite the International Olympic Committee's ban on other performance-enhancing substances. The problem with regulating caffeine in sports is that it's difficult to distinguish performance-enhancing quantities from typical intake from an athlete's daily diet. Everyday athletes using caffeine should do so with caution and realize that the advantages are only slight for most people.

In most of sports' recent doping scandals, there's one thing no one questions: the substances used. But next month—on sports' biggest stage—one known performance-enhancing drug will be allowed. In fact, you may have used it to boost your own performance as recently as this morning.

It's caffeine, and science supports its use as an ergogenic aid—in other words, a substance that enhances speed and stamina. Though Olympic officials once placed limits on its consumption, since 2004 athletes have been able to freely sip coffee or energy drinks, take caffeine pills, or chew caffeinated gum in search of that extra edge.

And recent research suggests up to three-fourths of the world's elite athletes do just that. Take now-retired Scottish cyclist Chris Hoy, a six-time gold medalist. He's so committed to his caffeine regimen that he reportedly lugged his own coffee machine and grinder to every competition, including the 2012 London Games.

How Caffeine Works

If you drink coffee, you're no stranger to caffeine's perks. The drug provides basically the same boost for athletes as it does for the office drone—delaying feelings of fatigue by blocking receptors for a sleep-related neurotransmitter called adenosine, says Louise Burke, Ph.D., head of sports nutrition at the Australian Institute of Sport and author of the book *Caffeine for Sports Performance.*

This means you can keep going for longer before you get tired, Burke says—whether you're driving a long-haul truck, prepping a PowerPoint, or going for the gold in the new Olympic sport, slopestyle.

The Beginnings of the Ban

Because of these benefits, Olympic officials first limited caffeine use in 1984, for the Los Angeles Summer Games. From then until 2004, athletes could be thrown out of competition if their urine contained more than 12 micrograms per milliliter of caffeine. The problem: These tests aren't precise—the amount of caffeine you consume that passes into your urine varies between individuals, ranging from 1 to 3 percent, Burke says. But you could probably take in about 9 milligrams (mg) per kilogram and still come in under this level, says Lawrence Spriet, Ph.D., a researcher at University of Guelph. If you're a 141-pound speedskater like J.R. Celski that'd be 576 mg, or about four Starbucks lattes.

In the 1980s, experts thought athletes required such megadoses of caffeine to see benefits. But recent research shows about the amount in a regular cup of coffee can do the trick, says Haemi Choi, M.D., a sports medicine specialist and a family physician at Loyola University Health System in Illinois. Though everyone responds differently, this amount has been shown to aid short-term, intense activities and improve endurance athletes' times by up to 3 percent—a margin that could certainly matter in Olympic-caliber competition, Burke says. But it isn't huge—it's about the same gain a marathon runner could expect from consuming carbohydrates during the race, she says. For that reason, it's often one small part of an athlete's overall strategy for doing his or her best, Spriet explains.

[Caffeine] poses far less long-term risk at effective doses than prohibited drugs like steroids and blood doping chemicals.

Lifting the Restriction

Evolving science has revealed that performance-enhancing doses of caffeine were practically indistinguishable from everyday use—that's why the World Anti-Doping Agency (WADA) moved caffeine off the list of prohibited substances. This list, reviewed annually, includes substances that enhance performance, present a health risk to the athlete, and "violate the spirit of sport," the code specifies.

Some would argue that caffeine meets these criteria, and some agencies—including the NCAA—still limit caffeine use. Besides concerns about unfair advantages, they cite caffeine's health risks at high doses, including gastrointestinal troubles, high blood pressure, anxiety, and irregular heartbeats that can eventually lead to death, Dr. Choi says.

But caffeine has obvious key differences from other banned drugs. For one, it's socially acceptable, Dr. Choi says. Plus, it poses far less long-term risk at effective doses than prohibited drugs like steroids and blood doping chemicals, Spriet says. So for Olympic athletes, caffeine remains on the "monitoring list" rather than the "prohibited list." This means that although athletes are still often tested for it in competition, they no longer face penalties for consuming it.

Fears that the lifted ban would trigger an explosion of misuse haven't materialized, either, although test results do suggest its consumption is on the rise, according to WADA spokesperson Ben Nichols. Still, the experts we consulted don't believe WADA will reinstitute a ban or limit anytime soon. "WADA has much bigger fish to fry with compounds that should be illegal as they can hurt people in the long run," Spriet says.

Get a Safe Jolt

By now, every athlete competing in the Winter Games has worked out a plan with coaches and nutritionists about whether—and how—to use caffeine, Spriet says. They're likely following these guidelines, which can also help you maximize your own caffeine habit.

Practice first. Caffeine affects everyone differently. Athletes fine-tune their doses and timing in training before using caffeine during high-stakes competition, Spriet says.

Time it right. Caffeine works best about an hour before a performance, Dr. Choi says. For later events, Burke advises athletes to adjust their regular consumption. In other words, instead of drinking a second cup of coffee in the afternoon, they should delay their morning dose so they don't overdo it.

Don't expect a miracle. "I work with hockey players and tell them it is just one additional thing that may allow the player to be the best they can be," Spriet says. In other words, it's no substitute for proper training, equipment, nutrition, and hydration.

11

Young Athletes Should Avoid Caffeine

Jay Williams

Jay Williams is a professor at Virginia Tech in the department of human nutrition, foods, and exercise.

Caffeine is a drug, a central nervous system stimulant that leads to physical and psychological dependence. Although there is evidence that caffeine can enhance performance in adults, it can also cause anxiety and nervousness and impair athletic ability. It is also a powerful diuretic, which can contribute to dehydration during sports. Particularly for young athletes, the risks of using caffeine far outweigh the potential benefits.

Energy drinks have become widely popular in the athletic community. In past years, ingestion [of caffeine] was primarily through coffee, tea and some sodas. Since most young athletes don't care for coffee or tea, their use of caffeine was limited. However, the introduction of so-called "energy drinks" have widened the access to caffeine. Sales of these beverages have increased. More and more brands appear on store shelves as they have become quite attractive to teens, athletes and non-athletes.

This raises several important questions: Are these beverages safe for young players to consume? Does the caffeine actually improve soccer performance?

Jay Williams, "Does Caffeine Enhance Player Performance?" National Soccer Coaches Association of America, April 22, 2014. NSCAA.com. © 2014 National Soccer Coaches Association of America. All rights reserved. Reproduced by permission.

Caffeine and Health

Answers to these questions are complicated. Here we take a look at the scientific evidence related to caffeine use and its effects on both performance and player health. In the research community, there is considerable debate as to whether or not caffeine is a true ergogenic [enhances performance] aid. A number of factors make caffeine research sometimes difficult to interpret. These include individual tolerances to the drug, the history of caffeine use, the doses provided and the type of activity studied. Nevertheless, there is evidence to suggest that caffeine may aid some types of performances but hinder others. There is also considerable evidence that dependence on caffeine as a method to improve performance may ultimately lead to long-term decrements in both performance and overall health, particularly in the young athlete.

Caffeine is one of the most widely consumed drugs in the world. It is found in a number of foods and beverages. If a commercial product contains caffeine, the US Food and Drug Administration requires [the manufacturer] to list it as an ingredient. This is usually found in the list of ingredients located near the bottom of the nutrition label. However, since caffeine is not considered a nutrient, the amount contained is not required. That information can be found on one of several websites. A few examples: A typical cup (8oz) of coffee may contain 75–150mg [milligrams] whereas some sodas (12 oz) and chocolates (1 oz) may contain 25–60 mg of caffeine. Caffeine may also be found in several over-the-counter pain medications, stimulants, weight loss supplements and cold/allergy drugs (30–200mg). Energy drinks contain substantial amounts of caffeine. A typical 16oz energy drink contains about 140–170mg while some may contain well over 300mg. Also, new energy mints, gums and chews contain caffeine ranging from about 5–40mg per piece. It is easy to see that caffeine is widely accessible to players of all ages.

Caffeine is classified as a central nervous system (CNS) stimulant. It is most often used to increase arousal and alertness and to offset mental and physical fatigue. It also affects the cardiovascular, pulmonary and neuromuscular systems. A number of athletes and coaches consider caffeine to be an ergogenic aid. That is, its use may improve athletic performance. Caffeine was first placed on the International Olympic Committee (IOC) banned substance list in 1962, removed in 1972 then added it back in 1984. In 2003, the World Anti-Doping Agency (WADA) removed caffeine as a prohibited substance, considering it only a "mild stimulant". It does remain a part of their Monitoring Program. The NCAA [National Collegiate Athletic Association] lists caffeine as a banned substance if urine levels exceed 15ug/ml [microgram per milliliter]. This is a high level. A 70 kg [kilogram] athlete (154 lbs) would need to take in 600–700mg to approach that level. The same player drinking a cup of strong coffee would show urine caffeine levels between 4–5 ug/ml. Thus, moderate amounts of caffeine like that found in coffee or energy drinks must be considered a legal ergogenic aid.

The well-know jitters caused by caffeine markedly reduce steadiness and can severely affect fine motor skills and precise movements . . . especially if high amounts of caffeine are consumed.

Caffeine's effects on the neuromuscular system and on strength and power activities are somewhat confusing. Laboratory studies on muscle tissue show that caffeine increases muscle strength. However, the effective concentrations used in these animal studies were excessive, often 100–500 times higher than blood levels found in humans even after excessive caffeine consumption. In our research, we found that caffeine ingestion by humans (~300 mg) has virtually no influence on muscular strength or power. Other studies also show little or no effect as well.

On the other hand, many studies show that caffeine decreases reaction, decision and movement times due to its arousal effects on the CNS. This effect might prove beneficial in a sport like soccer where rapid reactions to an opponent's movement are important. It should be pointed out caffeine can also negatively affect movement control. The well-know jitters caused by caffeine markedly reduce steadiness and can severely affect fine motor skills and precise movements. This could hinder a player's technical performance, especially if high amounts of caffeine are consumed.

An additional effect of caffeine consumption is on fuel utilization during prolonged exercise. In general, muscle uses two substrates for energy production—glucose and free fatty acids (FFAs). Glucose is found in the blood and stored in the muscle as glycogen. FFAs are stored in fat depots in various locations. During an intense match, performance can be limited by the availability of muscle glycogen and blood glucose. Because caffeine elevates FFAs in the blood, the muscle can use them as a fuel source. This tends to spare muscle glycogen and helps maintain blood glucose so that performance is better maintained. Studies on cyclists, swimmers and marathoners show that moderate caffeine consumption (100–200mg) can increase exercise duration and may lower finish times. Thus, in regards to long-term endurance performance, caffeine may be beneficial.

As for soccer, there have been several recent studies on the effects of caffeine on performance during simulated matches. In these studies, moderate amounts of caffeine are given 60 minutes prior to exercise. In general, these studies show that physical performance, especially during the later stages of the match may be improved. This includes sprinting (both speed and number of sprints), jumping ability and agility. Ratings of perceived exertion seem to be maintained as well. This applies to both male and female players. As for technical performance, the results are mixed. Dribbling, passing and receiving abilities are marginally improved in some studies and unaffected in others. Thus, based on the research studies, one must conclude that using caffeine can benefit match performance. In particular physical performance and effort near the end of a match may be enhanced.

Caffeine Risks

Because caffeine is widely available, it is imperative that both the athlete and coach fully understand the risks and benefits to both athletic performance and player. While caffeine is a naturally occurring substance and is found in many common foods and beverages, it is also a very potent drug and should always be treated as such. Thus, before arriving at a decision to use caffeine or not, one must consider a few cautionary words.

Unfortunately, many athletes feel that if some [caffeine] is good, more must be better.

First, it is well known that caffeine users can develop a physiological dependency. Over time, as caffeine is used on a regular basis, the beneficial effects often diminish. Moreover, headaches, fatigue, irritability and nausea typically occur in caffeine-dependent individuals when they do not have access to the drug. Psychological dependence can develop as well. An athlete who takes caffeine and has an outstanding match may soon feel that caffeine is required in order to compete. Without it, performance will suffer. Thus, using caffeine to enhance performance can lead a player down a slippery slope towards both physiological and psychological dependence. In these cases, the short-term, positive benefits of caffeine might very well be outweighed by the long-term side effects and dependency.

Second, caffeine can have a number of additional unwanted side effects. Even moderate amounts of caffeine can cause anxiety, nervousness and the jitters in some players, all of which can dramatically impair performance. Caffeine may induce gastrointestinal discomfort as well as cardiac arrhythmias and elevated blood pressure. It is also a powerful diuretic that can trigger the need to urinate. For healthy adults, these side effects are not life threatening but can make the athlete quite uncomfortable and impair performance. As for young players, there is very little research into the short- or long-term effects of caffeine in children or adolescents. It is quite possible that some young athletes may be more susceptible to psychological and cardiovascular complications. In addition, sleep patterns may be disrupted. These effects can be magnified since young players, who are smaller than their adult counterparts, often consume more caffeine per body weight.

Third, a key problem with caffeine use is the dosage. Studies show that 3–4 mg/kg taken 60 minutes before exercise is most effective. For a 70 kg player (154 lbs) this equals 210–280 mg or two 8 oz cups of coffee. Unfortunately, many athletes feel that if some is good, more must be better. However, more than 4 mg/kg offer no added benefit. More likely, that amount of caffeine will be detrimental, resulting in anxiety, inability to focus as well as raising the risk of cardiovascular problems.

The bottom line, for healthy, adult players, caffeine (~3 mg/kg), taken an hour before playing may improve performance throughout the match. The positive effects may be enhanced if caffeine is taken with a carbohydrate supplement. However, players should understand that some athletes will likely respond differently than others. Some will show improvement while others may not. Also, the risks of both physiological and psychological dependence may exceed any short-term gains derived from caffeine.

As for youth players, exercise physiologists and nutritionists all agree that these athletes should avoid the use of caffeine as an ergogenic aid. Athletes with cardiovascular or metabolic disorders such as hypertension and diabetes should avoid the use of caffeine as well. In these players, the potential side effects and health risks associated with repeated use clearly outweigh any possible benefits.

12

Children Can Safely Consume Some Coffee

Afdeza Monir

Afdeza Monir is a contributor to Malaysian Digest.

Many parents would not consider giving coffee to a young child; however, children drinking coffee is culturally acceptable in many parts of the world. Some scientists believe that, in moderation, coffee is perfectly fine for children and could help them perform better at school. Using caffeine in moderation is key to avoiding side effects and long-term health problems, but small amounts are not harmful for children.

Have you heard of 'beanie babies?' If you answered—plush toys filled with cotton and plastic pellets, you are wrong.

'Beanie babies' would possibly be the new term for children who actually drink coffee (yes, you read that right), and start drinking the beverage before the age of 5. These children usually come from families where coffee consumption is a cultural norm.

Cultural Norms

Latin American cultures especially are well-known for giving children coffee with milk at an early age as a warm drink served with breakfast.

Toddlers in Brazil consume milky coffee on a daily basis, and based on an interesting finding in the country, children who drink coffee with milk are less likely to have depression than other children.

It is also common in some communities like in Ethiopia and Cuba—as part of its culture, children are gradually eased into drinking coffee. In Croatia, as part of family or social gatherings, parents serve their little ones coffee with milk.

No studies have shown that coffee in reasonable amounts is in any way harmful to children.

Naturally, most parents would feel pious and refuse to give their children coffee at a young age. But according to Vanderbilt University research scientist, Dr. Tomas DePaulis, who published his own study on coffee, many parents who keep their kids as far away from coffee as possible could be wrong.

He claims coffee in moderation isn't bad for children and, like adults, it can help improve concentration and may help them do a little better on tests for this reason.

Pablo Dubois, of the International Coffee Organisation, echoed the same. He says, "One of the key things is it effectively dulls the addiction centres of the brain. If coffee is given to children, it could lead to them being less susceptible to alcohol and hard drugs in later life."

In fact, no studies have shown that coffee in reasonable amounts is in any way harmful to children.

The number of children drinking coffee is also increasing, and based on a recent study done by Boston University School of Medicine, "The rate of coffee consumption reported was 2.5 percent of children. At two years, that number increased to just above 15 percent, and the average daily consumption for these children was 1.09 ounces," according to Dr. Anne Merewood, an associate professor of pediatrics in the university.

The study also found that female infants had higher rates of coffee consumption than males.

Although there are no official guidelines for children's coffee consumption, there are of course, some potential health effects. Health professionals say that drinking coffee may be putting children at risk of addiction, obesity, diabetes, depression and, obviously, sleep problems.

Merewood notes that more research is required to measure the impact of coffee on toddlers.

"Given what the current data shows about the effects of coffee consumption among children and adolescents, additional research is needed to better determine the potential short- and long-term health implications of coffee consumption among this younger age group in Hispanic and other populations," she said.

A cup of coffee in the morning for your child may not be so bad after all, however, limiting caffeine consumption is key. And having said that, we should never forget that caffeine is also present in readily available things like soft drinks and chocolate.

13

Coffee Is Not Healthy for Children

Elyse Glickman

Elyse Glickman is an ongoing contributor to numerous publications, including The Jewish Journal, Tribe, *and* Taste & Travel, *and is the food and travel editor for* C-Suite Quarterly.

Researchers credit coffee consumption with numerous health benefits, including a lower mortality rate and increased mental focus and mental health. However, these benefits do not extend to children. Particularly in younger children, coffee and caffeine need to be avoided. Caffeine can act as an appetite suppressant and interfere with the consumption of needed nutrients, and it is toxic to several organs in the growing body. Parents should remember that caffeine is a drug, and even soft drinks and chocolate, which often contain caffeine, should be consumed by children in moderation.

Frapped, whipped, blended or heated, coffee has stirred up some popularity among an increasingly younger generation of fans, along with a touch of controversy on its benefits: What's good in theory for one generation could be bad for another.

A recent coffee study reported in *The New England Journal of Medicine* certainly adds to its appeal among people 50 and older. In conjunction with the AARP [formerly known as the American Association of Retired Persons], researchers from the National Institutes of Health followed more than 400,000 healthy men and women between the ages of 50 and 71.

Neal D. Freedman, lead author of the study and an investigator with the division of cancer epidemiology and genetics at the National Cancer Institute, in Rockville, Md., found the more coffee study participants drank, the lower their mortality risk tended to be.

Kids and Caffeine

However, the debate percolates on about whether or not teens and kids should be exposed to coffee and its caffeinated side effects. Before the charge of the Red Bull, and a herd of other energy drinks, teens and kids were starting to get a kick out of coffee in its many forms, thanks to both the baristas and the marketers behind Starbucks and other high-profile chains.

For nearly two decades, the plain "morning Joe" necessary to fuel many adult souls through a long day's work has evolved into a phenomenon that appeals to people of many ages and many palates.

Coffee may negatively affect a child's nutrition, possibly replacing nutrient-dense foods such as milk.

Though mom-and-pop coffee shops prevalent in college towns and chic neighborhoods played a role early on in the trend (remember "Central Perk" from the definitively '90s television series *Friends*?), the buzz on what's new can be found as closely as the run-of-the-mill supermarket, where coffee shops are now operated inside either independently or by the markets themselves.

If it's OK for adults, what about their kids? The experts have varied opinions.

Dr. Tomas DePaulis, a Vanderbilt University research scientist who recently published his own study on coffee, says that parents who keep their kids as far away from coffee as possible could be doing them a disservice.

He says coffee in moderation isn't bad for kids and, as with adults, it can help improve concentration and may help children do a little better on tests for this reason, he claims. He also points to another coffee study in Brazil that suggests that kids who drink coffee with milk are less likely to have depression than other children.

On the other hand, the National Institutes of Health [NIH], which ironically also was involved in Freedman's study of coffee's impact on people over 50, found that "a child's caffeine consumption should be closely monitored."

The NIH findings suggest coffee may negatively affect a child's nutrition, possibly replacing nutrient-dense foods such as milk.

A child may also eat less because caffeine acts as an appetite suppressant, according to the NIH study. Restriction or prohibition of coffee may also be a wise move when you look at children who are hyperactive or have other behavior-related disorders, it added.

Philadelphia native Dr. Charles Shubin says the coffee question recently came up on a visit to the area when his two young grandsons wanted to try a sip.

As the director of pediatrics at Mercy Family Care in Baltimore [Maryland], Shubin offers some very strong arguments about why children should not drink coffee; the biggest is that caffeine is a drug, albeit a legal one.

"Though caffeine is OK in moderation for adults, you should not introduce kids to coffee until they can fully grasp the concept of moderation," insists Shubin. "This usually happens in the middle of adolescence. Based on emotional development, in girls it would be 11 to 12, and for boys it would be two years older, because they need to be in a place psychologically where they can take responsibility for themselves."

Some may counter that children are exposed to coffee early in Latin American and European cultures the way they are exposed to beer and wine. If they are exposed to "adult" drinks early, they may develop the tools to handle them responsibly, goes the argument.

Shubin, however, counters that although it has been said that France and Germany may have fewer alcohol problems in their teen population compared to American teens (who, of course, can't legally touch it until they are 21), health studies in those countries tell a different story, with higher incidence of liver difficulties and other illnesses that may occur later in life due to prolonged exposure.

"One thing that's a common problem with telling kids 'no' is that when you prohibit something, it becomes more desirable," acknowledges Shubin. "We tell some kids not to drink coffee, only to discover they are going to find a way to do it, especially teens.

"It is more important to consider health factors, however. Caffeine is a drug, and it's a drug with significant potential toxicity that can affect the heart, the brain and other parts of the body. Kidneys, for example, can be affected as caffeine is a diuretic and it is something we should not have young or growing children exposed to."

Shubin adds that "going out for coffee" socially is an adult behavior, just like "going out for cocktails." While coffee is available legally, parents need to take responsibility, and he maintains the medical position that kids need to be raised healthy, which, in turn, means they should be raised without exposure to or [under] the influence of drugs, even if they are legal like caffeine or liquor.

But caffeine is present in readily available things like soft drinks and chocolate. Yes, but even there, overdoing it may involve consequences. Concludes Shubin: "Prohibiting coffee is not just an opportunity for a teachable moment with kids, but also adults. We all really need to be aware about what we do to our bodies when we make a choice to eat or drink certain things, and be aware of what is not so good for us if we go overboard."

14

Caffeinated Energy Drinks Are Dangerous for Young Children

Kathleen Doheny

Kathleen Doheny is a reporter for HealthDay.

Energy drinks contain substantially more caffeine than a cup of coffee, making them dangerous for children. Their consumption can cause certain side effects, including seizures and heart problems, and are responsible for numerous calls to poison control centers. Although the beverage industry states that they do not market these products to underage consumers, it's clear that the drinks are getting into the hands of young children. Everyone needs to work together to ensure that children do not have access to these dangerous beverages.

The potential dangers of energy drinks, those highly caffeinated beverages that promise to stave off sleepiness, are well known, but a new study suggests that even young children are at risk.

Although the target markets for energy drinks are typically teens and young adults, more than 40 percent of reports to U.S. poison control centers in a three-year period involved children under the age of 6, said study author Dr. Steven Lipshultz, pediatrician-in-chief at Children's Hospital of Michigan, in Detroit.

"About half of the calls to the national poison control data system for caffeinated energy drinks related to unintentional exposure for children less than 6," he noted. In more serious cases, seizures and heart problems were reported, the study found.

Typically, Lipshultz said, a young child finds the drink in the refrigerator and consumes it. "They didn't go into 7-11 and say 'I want to buy an energy drink,'" he said.

Lipshultz is to present his findings Sunday [November 16, 2014] at the American Heart Association annual meeting in Chicago. Studies presented at medical meetings are viewed as preliminary until published in a peer-reviewed journal.

Caffeine and Children's Health

For the study, Lipshultz and his colleagues analyzed data from the American Association of Poison Control Center's National Poison Data System. They looked for information about calls concerning energy drink exposures to 55 different poison control centers in the system.

The researchers examined data from October 2010 to September 2013. Before 2010, Lipshultz said, the system did not track energy drinks.

Some energy drinks have up to 400 milligrams (mg) of caffeine per serving . . . compared to about 100 mg or 150 mg in a typical cup of coffee.

The findings, he said, show that exposure to energy drinks is a continuing health problem. In 2011, after Lipshultz' previous research pointed out the dangers of energy drinks, the American Academy of Pediatrics said that energy drinks have no place in the diets of children.

Over the time period studied, there were more than 10,000 cases of energy drink exposure, with more than 5,000 being single substance exposures with contents that could be identified. Of those, more than 40 percent involved children under the age of 6.

Among all reports of major problems, more than 50 percent involved cardiovascular problems and more than half included neurologic problems such as seizures.

Some energy drinks have up to 400 milligrams (mg) of caffeine per serving, Lipshultz said, compared to about 100 mg or 150 mg in a typical cup of coffee.

Poisoning by caffeine can occur at levels higher than 400 mg a day in adults, he said, and above 100 mg a day in teens. For children under 12, 2.5 milligrams per every 2.2 pounds of body weight can be a danger, he said.

A group representing beverage makers said energy drinks are in no way intended for consumption by the very young.

"Leading energy drink makers voluntarily place advisory statements on energy drink packaging stating that energy drinks are not intended for children," the American Beverage Association said in a statement. "They also have voluntarily pledged not to market these products to children or sell them in K-12 schools."

The group also noted that, "based on the most recent government data reported in the journal *Pediatrics*, children under 12 have virtually no caffeine consumption from energy drinks."

When the drinks are mixed with alcohol, the problems can be worse, Lipshultz found. Those with underlying heart problems can be at higher danger.

"The findings of this study are unfortunately not surprising given the heavy marketing of sports and energy drinks to youth, and national data that have provided evidence these beverages are being consumed by young children," said Nicole Larson, senior research associate at the University of Minnesota.

The serious health consequences of consumption by young children described in the new study are concerning, she said. The findings point to the need for parents, health professionals, coaches and teachers to continue their efforts to reduce the marketing and availability of energy drinks to children.

Larson reminds parents that the American Academy of Pediatrics recommends against the consumption of energy drinks by children. Instead, she said, parents can help their children to adopt healthy hydration habits "focusing on water to replenish fluids after exercise and the consumption of nutritious beverages such as low-fat milk at meals."

15

Caffeine Products
May Be Dangerous

David Bruser

David Bruser is part of the investigations team with The Star, *in Toronto, Canada.*

Caffeinated energy drinks can cause serious side effects and are responsible for several deaths. The companies that produce the highly caffeinated beverages insist the drinks are intended for and marketed to adults and state there is no proof that their products caused fatalities. However, the drinks, which are especially popular with teens, have been connected to several overdoses. In 2011, Health Canada announced rules requiring product labels that contain caffeine content information as well as a health advisory.

Popular energy drinks are suspected to have caused the deaths of three teens—as well as serious side effects such as irregular heartbeat and amnesia in 35 other Canadians—since 2003, according to reports filed with Health Canada.

The three male teens, two 15-year-olds and an 18-year-old, died after drinking Red Bull, which appears in more side-effect reports than any other similar product.

In one of these cases, the death of a 15-year-old in 2006, Monster Energy was also consumed.

"I am not shocked to hear of the deaths that are coming to the surface now," said Jim Shepherd of Toronto, whose 15-

year-old son Brian died Jan. 6, 2008, after drinking a can of Red Bull during a paintball tournament. He collapsed at the awards banquet that night.

Shepherd said the coroner ruled Brian died from sudden arrhythmic death syndrome. He believes Red Bull contributed to his son's irregular heartbeat and death.

Health Canada and the energy drink companies said the side-effect reports show only a suspected connection between a product and side effect but no medical proof that one caused the other. (A report is the opinion of the consumer, pharmacist, doctor or nurse that a drug or energy drink is suspected to have caused a side effect.)

A Red Bull spokesperson referred questions to the Canadian Beverage Association, which represents energy and other drink companies.

"Because a product or ingredient is listed on an adverse events report it in no way confirms or even implies a causal link," said beverage association spokeswoman Stephanie Baxter. "There can be a multitude of items listed on each report and a full review of the event is required to determine which, if any, played a role."

Nova Scotia's professional doctors association asked the province earlier this year to ban the sale of the [caffeinated energy] drinks to people younger than 19.

More Deaths Linked to Energy Drinks

Last week [November 2012], reports emerged of 13 deaths in the U.S. possibly linked to 5-hour Energy, a caffeinated energy shot also sold in Canada.

The Star found five cases of Canadians suffering serious side effects suspected to have been caused by 5-hour Energy, including an 18-year-old who also consumed at least two other brands of energy drinks when he experienced "delusion" and a hallucination.

A spokeswoman for Living Essentials, the Michigan-based company that distributes 5-hour Energy, said in a statement last week that it takes reports of potential adverse reactions seriously and that it was not aware of any deaths proven to have been caused by the "energy shot intended for busy adults."

In Canada, some provinces are looking at putting limits on the sale of energy drinks. A New Brunswick private member's bill, which reached second reading earlier this year, would require stores that sell energy drinks to display warning signs with the drinks.

Nova Scotia's professional doctors association asked the province earlier this year to ban the sale of the drinks to people younger than 19.

"That would exclude children and youth because we feel they're at particular risk of consumption of high amounts of caffeine," said Dr. John Finley, president of Doctors Nova Scotia.

The energy drinks include, among other ingredients, caffeine, taurine, and vitamins B6 and B12. On the cans, near the mention of "recommended dose" and list of "medicinal" ingredients, are cautions that the drink is not recommended for children or pregnant women.

In each of the serious side-effect reports where energy drinks are mentioned as the suspected cause, the consumer either went to the hospital, suffered a disability or life-threatening condition, or died.

Three-quarters of the reports found by *The Star* were filed in just the last few years.

California-based Monster Beverage Corporation said its Monster Energy drinks—listed as the suspected cause in six serious side-effect reports—"comply fully with all laws and regulations in each of the more than 70 countries in which they are sold."

A company spokesperson told *The Star*: "From the information that we have seen, there is no causation in any of these (Canadian) reports. There is no real link."

The company points out that the labelling says the energy drinks are not recommended for children, pregnant women or people sensitive to caffeine.

The Canadian Beverage Association said that advertising and marketing for the products target people between 18 and 34. "We do not target teens, we don't sell energy drinks in schools," said association spokeswoman Baxter.

The association said that it hired third-party experts to review the Canadian side-effect reports associated with energy drinks. "They came back (in 2011) and basically said there was no sound scientific evidence and that it wasn't possible to draw any conclusions regarding them," Baxter told *The Star*.

One of the reports was prepared for the beverage association by Dr. Jeffrey Carson, who wrote: "Any potential link between the death of the two 15-year-olds and possible energy drink consumption requires additional evaluation. Both cases were determined to be 'unassessable' by Health Canada because of lack of information."

The document was prepared before the third Canadian death.

Other energy drinks listed in Health Canada's database as the suspected cause of side effects are Rockstar Energy and NOS.

"We are not aware of any reports of fatalities associated with consuming any of our company's energy drink brands. We take the safety and quality of the beverages we sell very seriously," a spokesperson for Coca-Cola, the Canadian distributor of NOS, which appears in four serious side-effect reports, told *The Star*.

Rockstar Energy did not respond to several messages left by *The Star*.

Serious Side Effects

Of the 38 Canadian cases of serious side effects suspected to have been caused by energy drinks, *The Star* found 15 cases that involved people 19 years old and younger.

The Star also found:

- In 19 cases, a Red Bull drink was listed as the suspected cause of the side effect. In three of those reports, alcohol was also listed as the suspected cause of the side effect.

- 13 consumers experienced palpitations.

- Amnesia and convulsions were each cited in three reports.

Health Canada is monitoring a U.S. Food and Drug Administration review of reports linked to 5-hour Energy, said Adam Gibson, interim director general of the natural health products directorate.

"Within the Canadian (5-hour Energy) reports, there were no deaths," he said. "So seeing deaths coming out of the U.S. is something we'd want to check ... obviously a death is something we take very seriously, or any serious adverse reaction."

Gibson said the Canadian reports of side effects suspected to have been caused by 5-hour Energy have been investigated, but said details of the investigation were not immediately available.

Health Canada says that under new rules announced in 2011, the drinks cannot exceed a certain amount of caffeine, and product labelling must include the caffeine level as well as an advisory not to mix the drink with alcohol.

"I really think they should ban the sale (of the drinks) to minors to protect them," said Brian's father, Jim Shepherd.

"There should be point-of-sale warning signage in the stores and these products should be in a separate area of the store."

Organizations to Contact

The editors have compiled the following list of organizations concerned with the issues debated in this book. The descriptions are derived from materials provided by the organizations. All have publications or information available for interested readers. The list was compiled on the date of publication of the present volume; the information provided here may change. Be aware that many organizations take several weeks or longer to respond to inquiries, so allow as much time as possible.

Academy of Nutrition and Dietetics
120 S. Riverside Plaza, Suite 2000, Chicago, IL   60606
(800) 877-1600
website: www.eatright.org

The Academy of Nutrition and Dietetics is the world's largest organization of food and nutrition professionals. The group strives to improve the nation's health and advance the profession of dietetics through research, education, and advocacy. The organization focuses on food and nutrition research and offers scholarships and awards. Its website, EatRight.org, contains numerous papers on managing a healthy, nutritionally sound vegetarian diet.

American Heart Association (AHA)
7272 Greenville Ave., Dallas, TX   75231
(800) 242-8721
website: www.heart.org

The American Heart Association (AHA) engages in a range of activities, including medical research, professional education, and patient education, to promote a world free of heart disease and stroke. The AHA website provides nutritional guidelines and information on physical activity, stress and weight management, and smoking, as well as a section devoted to caffeine and heart disease.

Centers for Disease Control and Prevention (CDC)

1600 Clifton Rd., Atlanta, GA   30333
(800) 232-4636
website: www.cdc.gov

As the health protection agency of the United States, the Centers for Disease Control and Prevention (CDC) promotes health and the prevention of disease, injury, and disability. To accomplish this mission, the CDC conducts critical research and provides health information to members of the healthcare and public safety community. The CDC website includes consumer health information on lifestyle diseases, such as heart disease and diabetes, as well as information about food safety and diet.

Health Canada

Tower A, Qualicum Towers, 2936 Baseline Rd.
Ottawa   O K1A OK9
   Canada
(866) 225-0709
website: www.hc-sc.gc.ca

Health Canada is the federal department responsible for helping Canadians maintain and improve their health. Health Canada relies on high-quality scientific research and conducts ongoing consultations with Canadians to determine long-term health-care needs. The agency encourages Canadians to take an active role in their health and issues publications, including *Canada's Food Guide to Healthy Eating.* Its website also contains information on caffeine as a food additive, caffeine and children, energy drinks, and other caffeine-related issues.

Institute for Scientific Information on Coffee (ISIC)

Basepoint Evesham, Crab Apple Way, Evensham
Worcestershire   WR11 1GP
+44 (0) 1386 764777
e-mail: info@coffeeandhealth.org
website: http://coffeeandhealth.org

The Institute for Scientific Information on Coffee (ISIC) is a nonprofit organization devoted to the study and disclosure of the science related to coffee and health. The organization's activities include the study of scientific matters, collection and evaluation of studies, support of independent scientific research on coffee and health, and dissemination of balanced coffee and health scientific evidence. ISIC's website, coffeeandhealth.org, contains links to the latest research, a blog, and additional resources.

US Department of Agriculture, Center for Nutrition Policy and Promotion (CNPP)
3101 Park Center Dr., 10th Floor, Alexandria, VA   22302
(703) 305-7600
website: www.cnpp.usda.gov

The Center for Nutrition Policy and Promotion (CNPP), within the US Department of Agriculture (USDA), works to improve the health of Americans by developing and promoting dietary guidance that links scientific research to the nutrition needs of consumers. The agency's website includes considerable information on such topics as nutrition, dietary guidelines, USDA food plans, and other issues.

US Department of Health and Human Services
Office of Disease Prevention and Health Promotion
200 Independence Ave. SW, Washington, DC   20201
(877) 696-6775
e-mail: odphpinfo@hhs.gov
website: http://health.gov

The Health.gov website, which publishes current dietary and physical activity guidelines for Americans, is coordinated by the Office of Disease Prevention and Health Promotion of the US Department of Health and Human Services. The website evaluates the strength of the evidence supporting each of the guidelines, provides detailed information on the nutrient content of various foods, and also addresses issues like diet-related chronic diseases and food safety.

US Food and Drug Administration (FDA)
5100 Paint Branch Pkwy., College Park, MD   20740
(888) 463-6332
website: www.fda.gov

The US Food and Drug Administration (FDA) is the government agency responsible for ensuring the quality and safety of all food and drug products sold in the United States. As such, the FDA regulates safety and truthful labeling of all food products, including dietary supplements (except for livestock and poultry, which are regulated by the US Department of Agriculture), venison and other game meat, bottled water, food additives, and infant formulas. FDA reports, as well as current information on food quality issues, are available at its website.

World Health Organization (WHO)
Avenue Appia 20, Geneva 27   1211
   Switzerland
+41 22 791 21 11
website: www.who.int

The role of the World Health Organization (WHO) is to direct and coordinate international health within the United Nations' system. WHO supports countries working to coordinate the efforts of multiple sectors of the government and partners, including foundations, civic organizations, and the private sector, to reach their health objectives and support their national health policies and strategies. The WHO health topic page on diet provides links to descriptions of activities, reports, publications, statistics, news, multimedia, and events.

Bibliography

Books

Stewart Lee Allen — *The Devil's Cup: A History of the World According to Coffee.* New York: Ballantine Books, 2003.

Charlotte Biltekoff — *Eating Right in America: The Cultural Politics of Food & Health.* Durham, NC: Duke University Press, 2013.

Stephen Braun — *Buzz: The Science and Lore of Alcohol and Caffeine.* New York: Oxford University Press, 1996.

Louise Burke, Ben Desbrow, and Lawrence Spriet — *Caffeine for Sports Performance.* Champaign, IL: Human Kinetics, 2012.

Murray Carpenter — *Caffeinated: How Our Daily Habit Helps, Hurts, and Hooks Us.* New York: Hudson Street Press, 2014.

Stephen Cherniske — *Caffeine Blues: Wake Up to the Hidden Dangers of America's #1 Drug.* New York: Warner Books, 1998.

Robert J. Davis — *Coffee Is Good for You: From Vitamin C and Organic Foods to Low-Carb and Detox Diets, the Truth About Diet and Nutrition Claims.* New York: Perigee Trade, 2012.

Ryan Reynold — *The Truth About Caffeine: The World's Most Consumed Drug.* Seattle, WA: CreateSpace, 2014.

Janelle Watkinson	*Caffeine Addiction Gone—A Beginner's Guide to Overcoming Caffeine Addiction.* Portland, OR: CreateSpace, 2014.
Bennett Alan Weinberg	*The Caffeine Advantage: How to Sharpen Your Mind, Improve Your Physical Performance, and Achieve Your Goals—the Healthy Way.* New York: The Free Press, 2002.
Bennett Alan Weinberg and Bonnie K. Bealer	*The World of Caffeine: The Science and Culture of the World's Most Popular Drug.* London: Routledge, 2001.

Periodicals and Internet Sources

Erin Brodwin and Kevin Loria	"What Caffeine Does to Your Body and Brain," *Business Insider*, April 23, 2015. www.businessinsider.com.
Bonnie Brost	"Nutrition: Youths at Risk from Caffeine in 'Energy' Drinks," *Duluth News Tribune*, May 12, 2015.
Aaron E. Carroll	"More Consensus on Coffee's Benefits Than You Might Think," *New York Times*, May 11, 2015.
Linda Carroll	"Kids and Caffeine May Be a Dangerous Combination, New Study Suggests," *Today*, June 16, 2014. www.today.com.

Center for Science in the Public Interest — "Petition to Ban the Retail Distribution of Pure and Highly Concentrated Caffeine Sold in Powder Form as a Dietary Supplement," December 9, 2014. http://cspinet.org.

Geoffrey Kabat — "Natural Does Not Mean Safe," *Slate*, November 26, 2012. www.slate.com.

Jamie Lampros — "Is Caffeinated Water the New Energy Drink?," *Standard Examiner*, May 1, 2015.

Douglas Main — "Caffeine During Pregnancy Nearly Doubles Childhood Obesity Risk," *Newsweek*, May 8, 2015. www.newsweek.com.

NorthJersey.com — "NJ Legislature Considers Outlawing Powdered Caffeine," May 14, 2015. www.northjersey.com.

Caroline Picard — "12 Reasons You Need to Drink Coffee Every Single Day," *Good Housekeeping*, April 24, 2015.

Ross Pomeroy — "You're Drinking Caffeine All Wrong," *Real Clear Politics*, May 13, 2015. www.realclearpolitics.com.

Casey Seidenberg — "Why Caffeine Is Bad for Your Kids," *Washington Post*, May 23, 2012.

Joseph Stromberg — "Coffee Naps Can Improve Performance," *Vox*, August 28, 2014. www.vox.com.

Joseph Stromberg   "This Is How Your Brain Becomes Addicted to Caffeine," *Smithsonian Magazine*, August 9, 2013.

Lisa Sugarman   "It Is What It Is: It's Not Called a Caffeine High for Nothing," *Journal Star*, April 20, 2015.

Chris Woolston   "The Healthy Skeptic: Is Caffeine an Effective Weight-Loss Aid?," *Los Angeles Times*, January 9, 2012.

Judith J. Wurtman   "Can You Caffeinate Yourself to a Lower Weight?," *Huffington Post*, September 12, 2012. www.huffingtonpost.com.

Liberty Zabala and Laura McVicker   "Using Caffeine to Help Premature Babies Survive," NBC SanDiego, February 18, 2015. www.nbcsandiego.com.

Index

A

abuse-related problems, 33

addiction.com website, 30–34

addiction concerns, 30–34, 46

adrenaline release, 44–45

Advanced Healthcare Network, 47–51

alcohol-induced impairment, 39

Alert Energy Caffeine Gum, 28

alertness and safety effects, 37–39

Alzheimer's disease, 47–51

American Academy of Pediatrics, 80, 82

American Association of Poison Control Center, 80

American Association of Retired Persons (AARP), 74

American Beverage Association, 81

American Heart Association, 80

American Journal of Clinical Nutrition, 12

American Journal of Medicine, 26

American Medical Association Council on Scientific Affairs, 14

American Psychiatric Association, 30, 33

anhedonia, 42

Annals of Neurology (Ascherio), 11

anxiety disorders, 31

Appetite magazine, 12

Arendash, Gary, 49, 50

Ascherio, Alberto, 11

athletic benefits of caffeine

avoidance by young athletes, 64–70

doping concerns, 60–63

overview, 57–58

Attention deficit hyperactivity disorder (ADHD), 52–55

Australian Institute of Sport, 61

B

Baxter, Stephanie, 84

Baylor College of Medicine, 7

Bedford, Michael, 21

bipolar disorder, 42

Boston University School of Medicine, 72

Bradberry, Travis, 43–46

breast cancer protection, 50

Bruser, David, 83–88

Burke, Louise, 61

C

caffeine

as addictive, 30–34, 46

Alzheimer's disease, 47–51

Attention deficit hyperactivity disorder, 52–55

death by, 16–19

glucose/caffeine synergy, 40, 54, 67

health benefits, 10–15

introduction, 7–9

Parkinson's Disease, 11, 50

as performance enhancing, 56–59

H

Hansen's Energy, 24

Harvard School of Public Health, 12

Harvard University, 13

health benefits of caffeine
  of caffeine, 10–15
  cancer risks, 13–14
  cognitive functioning improvements, 11–12
  concerns/complications over, 14–15
  depression, 12
  diabetes, 12–13
  energy drinks, 65–68
  Parkinson's Disease, 11

Health Byrd Alzheimer's Institute, 48

Health Canada, 83, 84, 86

health concerns, 26–28, 68–70

hepatitis, 19

hepatocellular carcinoma, 13

high blood pressure, 14

homeopathy, 14

Hoy, Chris, 61

I

Institute for Scientific Information on Coffee, 35–42

insulin resistance, 13, 15

International Coffee Organisation, 72

International Olympic Committee (IOC), 57, 66

Ireland, Jeanne, 25

J

Jackson, John, 16, 18

JAMA (Journal of the American Medical Association), 11

Johns Hopkins University Medical School, 44

Journal of Alzheimer's Disease, 48

Journal of the National Cancer Institute, 13

K

Kuzma, Cindy, 60–63

L

Larson, Nicole, 81

Latin American coffee culture, 71–72

Leung, W.W., 13

Lipshultz, Steven, 79–81

liver disease, 14

Living Essential, 85

Loyola University Health System, 62

M

Maleki, Nancy, 10–15

Marcus, Donald M., 7

memory effects, 39–40, 53

Mercy Family Care, 76

Merewood, Anne, 72–73

methylated xanthine, 20

mild cognitive impairment (MCI), 48, 50

MJA (Medical Journal of Australia), 17